the true story of the
last eyewitness

# The Gospel of John

Retold by Chris Seay
with devotional commentary

A SCRIPTURE PROJECT TO REDISCOVER THE STORY OF THE BIBLE

## Thomas Nelson
*Since 1798*

NASHVILLE   DALLAS   MEXICO CITY   RIO DE JANEIRO   BEIJING

www.thomasnelson.com

# CONTRIBUTORS

**Scriptures and commentary by:**

Chris Seay

**Scholarly review by:**

David Capes
Alan Culpepper
Peter Davids
Jack Wisdom

**Editorial review by:**

James F. Couch, Jr.
Maleah Bell
Marilyn Duncan
Amanda Haley
Kelly Hall
Merrie Noland

the
voice™

A SCRIPTURE PROJECT TO REDISCOVER THE STORY OF THE BIBLE

# FOREWORD

Everybody likes to hear good news. Good news enlivens us and fills us with joy, at least for a time. It turns the sky a deeper shade of blue. It makes the leftovers taste as if they were hot off the grill. Good news can shorten a long, hard day at work or school and can make our world appear safer and more secure. The only thing better than hearing good news is sharing good news with people you love.

*The Voice Revealed* is a book of good news. Not the kind of good news that gives you a temporary boost, but the kind that can and will transform your life as faith takes hold and grows within you. This book traces the words and actions of Jesus the Liberating King in the most distinctive account of His journey. If you are like most people, from time to time you wrestle with ultimate questions, questions about the existence of God and your purpose in this world. So we at the Ecclesia Bible Society and Thomas Nelson have come together to share some good news. It may not answer all your questions today, but it will lead you to some new questions and, in our experience, change your life and direction. We want to invite you to read *The Voice Revealed* and allow this amazing story to wash over you, captivate you, and change you. You may have read the Gospel according to John before, but you've never experienced a retelling of it like this. We promise you won't be disappointed.

This Gospel was written so we could experience something of what it would be like to spend time with Jesus. John is the only friend and follower of Jesus who recounts his experience with the most significant figure in the history of the world in such a deeply personal way. He does not just record what Jesus said and where He went—John tells this story as a memoir with the kind of details that activate our spiritual imaginations. The picture of true faith painted in John's Gospel is all about love, service, kindness, and forgiveness.

To give some history and context to the Gospel, we've provided a running commentary written in first person, as if it were written by John. Our starting point is this: What would it be like to be the last person on earth who remembers the sound of

Jesus' voice, the manner of His walk, and the curve of His smile? Our purpose is simply to draw you into the characters and the events of the story and ultimately to invite you to follow Jesus and become His witness too. We often read biblical passages quickly and give little attention to the emotions and details of the events, so in this book we hope to slow the pace just a bit and hear the voice of John, the last eyewitness, at the end of his life. The story is his, and we are his audience.

John's uniquely personal perspective on Jesus in his Gospel reached its maturity on an island known as Patmos, where John had been banished. If you know the way God works, then you realize that being deported, banished, captured, jailed, or enslaved is just another way of saying that you are being sent by God on a mission. That's how God orchestrates the spread of His redemptive narrative. You see, in God's economy, good news often comes of age in rather harsh circumstances. In John's case, this was a barren piece of real estate jutting out of the Aegean Sea (off of modern Turkey's western coast). But the beloved disciple, as the Gospel calls him, arrived in this new land and culture a free man. He looked around, took a deep breath, and started a church. And in so doing, he began the subtle but substantial work of transforming his world. This is what attracted the attention of the powers-that-be in his day who liked the world the way it was and decided that John, like Jesus before him, was a dangerous character.

The church John started did not have a steeple, pulpit, baptistry, finance committee, or parking lot. But have no doubt that this was a church in the truest sense—a Christ-filled community with celebrations and dinner parties, shared finances, house meetings, and habitual gatherings on the beach around the fire. John would sit nearest to the fire, and the community would gather around him to listen to his stories and ask questions. He was their founder, their leader, and they hung on his every word.

John spoke the story of Jesus, our Liberating King, in beautiful detail and prose. Thankfully, the beloved disciple and his community of believers eventually put pen to papyrus to ensure that the story would be perpetually retold until Jesus returns to live out the sequel. They close this narrative record with an insightful apology:

> There are so many other things that Jesus said and did; and if these accounts were also written down, the books could not be contained in the entire cosmos (21:25).

This story is interactive. As in all the **Voice** products, we've employed a few features to make the experience of reading *The Voice Revealed* more rewarding. First, you'll notice that we place the dialogues in a distinctive screenplay format. This makes it easier to become a part of the story and, if you choose, to read or perform it aloud. Second, we use italicized words and phrases to provide additional information and details so that the historical and cultural differences between our worlds will not seem so great. Third, we punctuate the text with brief essays and commentaries that we've composed. You'll see these in boxes situated throughout the story. These essays are also designed to draw out the meaning of the text and to draw you deeper into the story.

We encourage you to hear His Voice, enter His story, consider His claims, and then decide for yourself what you will do with Him and for Him. He is inviting you into a journey of faith that will lead to the most authentic life you will ever know. He is calling you into His *ecclesia,* a community of deeply flawed but forgiven, called-out characters committed to the journey. So you will not be alone. His way is not "Easy Street" or "Broad Way." His journey will take some of you to the ends of the earth—but at the end, you'll find life, purpose, meaning, and true wealth. So come into the story, smell the mixture of the salty air and the billows of smoke floating from the bonfire, and hear the last eyewitness.

—Ecclesia Bible Society

*M*y name is John. My father's name was Zebedee. We made our living by fishing on the Sea of Galilee. I am the last eyewitness to the life of Jesus. All the rest are gone; some long gone. Many died years ago, tragically young, the victims of Roman cruelty and persecution. For some reason, Jesus chose me to live to be an old man. In fact, some in my community have taken to calling me "the elder."

I am the inspiration behind the Fourth Gospel. These are my stories, recorded, told to you by my disciples. I'm proud of what they have done. Me? I've never done much writing. But the story is truly mine.

You see my hands. They've been hurting for the past 20 years now. I couldn't hold a pen even if I wanted to. Not that I was ever good at writing. I was a fisherman, so my hands were calloused. I could tie ropes, mend nets, and pull the oars, but never make a decent *xi* (Greek letter). So we used secretaries when we wanted to write. There was always a bright young man around it seems, ready to take a letter or help us put pen to papyrus.

My eyes are too weak to read anymore. I can't remember the last time I could see well enough to read a letter or even see the inscriptions. So one of the brothers (I call them my "little children") reads to me. They are all very gracious to me in my old age, compiling my stories, bringing me food, laughing at my jokes, and caring for my most intimate needs. Time is taking its toll on me though. I rarely have the energy to tell the old stories and preach entire sermons. Instead, I simply remind them of the Liberating King's most vital command, saying as loudly as I can, "Little children, love one another."

Jesus had this group of guys. He called us "the twelve." We traveled with Him, spent time with Him, ate with Him, and listened to Him talk about God's kingdom. We watched Him perform miracles. These weren't the tricks like you see in the market or attempts at magic you hear about at shrines. These were what I call "signs." Something was breaking into our darkness. These signs pointed to a greater reality most people didn't even know was there. In the other Gospels, they call them "miracles" or "works of power." We've decided to tell you about select signs because these, more than any, revealed the true glory of this man.

Jesus wanted us to be His family, a different kind of community. We figured it out later. By calling us "the twelve," Jesus was remembering the original twelve tribes of Israel while creating a new people of God. God was doing something new, like the prophets had promised. We were living at the center of history. From now on, every-thing would be different. This made us feel special, proud, and sometimes arrogant. We'd sometimes jockey for Jesus' attention. Even within the twelve some were closer to Jesus. He had this "inner circle" of sorts. I was part of it. Peter, Andrew, James, and I were with Jesus at times when the other fellows had to stay behind. I'm not sure why He picked me. Because of that, I knew He loved me and I would have a special place with Him.

Jesus also had other students. Not all of them stayed. Some came, and some went. I don't really know how many people in all. One time He sent out 70 of us to proclaim the good news and heal in His name. He even let women be His students. Most people don't know this, but women were among those who helped support us financially.[1] At a time when people said it was a shame for a man to be supported by women, Jesus took their help and took it gladly. But there were no women among the twelve. That was only right. In our day, women didn't travel with men who were not family. Scandal was always swirling around Jesus; He didn't want or need to fight that battle.

I've outlived all the rest of the twelve and His other fol-lowers. I can't tell you how lonely it is to be the last person

[1] Luke 8:3

with a memory, some would even say a fuzzy memory, of what Jesus looked like, the sound of His voice, the manner of His walk, the penetrating look in His eyes. All I can do is tell my story.

Others have written accounts of what happened among us. The other Gospels have faithfully portrayed the public Jesus. But I feel compelled to tell the story of the private Jesus. The others show us how Jesus preached and dealt with the multitudes. But I still remember the small group time with Jesus and the conversations He had with Nicodemus, the Samaritan woman, and the man born blind—I don't remember his name.

The other Gospels tell the tragedy and injustice of Jesus' death. Here was the single greatest man in history who was falsely accused; who was dragged before corrupt priests and a cruel Roman governor. He was condemned to death and crucified in a most hideous manner. On a human level, Jesus' arrest, condemnation, and crucifixion were tragedies of epic proportions. But the more this old man thinks about what happened, the more I understand now that Jesus' death was His greatest hour. Things seemed to spin out of control so quickly. One minute we were celebrating the Passover together in the upper room; the next we were running for our lives! I'm not sure who was to blame for what happened to Jesus. Envious priests? The Roman governor? But, in fact, He was in complete control. That's why I say the hour of His death was the hour of His greatest glory. That's why I think that when Jesus was lifted up on the cross, He became the means by which all people can come to God. The most vivid memory that lingers in this old man's mind is of Jesus up there on the cross. I can still see it like it was yesterday. His body—hanging halfway between heaven and earth, embracing the world—bridged the gap between God and humanity.

Now I want to be very clear. This is my story, but unlike

what you hear from most storytellers, this is completely true. I am giving you the testimony of an eyewitness. And like my brother disciples, I will swear upon my life that it is true.

## Chapter 1

[1]Before time itself was measured, the Voice was speaking. The Voice was and is God. [2]This *celestial* Voice remained ever present with the Creator; [3]His speech shaped the entire cosmos. *Immersed in the practice of creating,* all things that exist were birthed in Him. [4]His breath filled all things with a living, breathing light. [5]Light that thrives in the depths of darkness, *blazing through murky bottoms.* It cannot, and will not, be quenched.

[6]A man named John, who was sent by God, *was the first to clearly articulate the source of this unquenchable Light.* [7]This wanderer, *John who ritually cleansed,*[*] put in plain words the *elusive mystery of the Divine* Light that all might believe through him. *Because John spoke with power, many believed in the Light. Others wondered whether he might be the Light,* [8]but John was not the Light. He merely pointed to the Light; *and in doing so, he invited the entire creation to hear the Voice.*

[9]The true Light, who shines upon the heart of everyone, was coming into the cosmos. [10]*He does not call out from a distant place but draws near.* He enters our world, a world He made *and speaks clearly,* yet His creation did not recognize Him. [11]*Though the Voice utters only truth,* His own people, *who have heard the Voice before,* rebuff this inner calling and refuse to listen. [12]But those who *hear and* trust the beckoning of the Divine Voice and embrace Him, they shall be reborn as children of God, [13]He bestows this birthright not by human

---

* 1:7 Literally, immersed, to show repentance

power or initiative but by God's will. *Because we are born of this world, we can only be reborn to God by accepting His call.*

[14]The Voice *that had been an enigma in the heavens chose to* become human and live surrounded by His creations. We have seen Him. Undeniable splendor enveloped Him—the one true Son of God—*evidenced in* the perfect balance of grace and truth. [15]John, *the wanderer* who testified of the Voice, introduced Him. "This is the one I've been telling you is coming. He is much greater than I because He existed *long* before me." [16]Through this man we all receive *gifts of* grace beyond our imagination. *He is the Voice of God.* [17]You see, Moses gave us rules to live by, but Jesus the Liberating King offered the gifts of grace and truth *which make life worth living.* [18]God, unseen until now, is revealed in the Voice, God's only Son, *straight from* the Father's heart.

---

*B*efore Jesus came along, many thought John the Immerser might be the Liberating King. But when Jesus appeared in the wilderness, John pointed us to Him. The Immerser knew his place in God's redemptive plan. John the Immerser was a man sent from God, but Jesus is the Voice of God. John rejected any messianic claim outright. Jesus, though, accepted it with a smile, but only from a few of us—at least at first. Don't get me wrong, John was important, but he wasn't the Liberating King. He preached repentance. He told everybody to get ready for One greater to come along. The One who comes will immerse us in fire and power, he said. John even told some of his followers to leave him and go follow Jesus.

---

[19]The words of the Immerser were *gaining attention,* and many had questions, including Jewish religious leaders from Jerusalem. [28]Their entourage approached John in Bethany just beyond the Jordan River while he was cleansing* followers in water, *and bombarded him with questions:*

---

* 1:28 Literally, immersing, to show repentance
* 1:28 Verse 28 has been inserted here to help retain the continuity of events.

**Religious Leaders:** Who are you?

**John the Immerser:** [20]I'm not the Liberator, *if that is what you are asking.*

**Religious Leaders:** [21]*Your words sound familiar, like a prophet's.* Is that how we should address you? Are you the Prophet Elijah?

**John the Immerser:** No, I am not Elijah.

**Religious Leaders:** Are you the Prophet *Moses told us would come*?

**John the Immerser:** No.

*They continued to press John, unsatisfied with the lack of information.*

**Religious Leaders:** [22]Then tell us who you are and what you are about because everyone is asking us, *especially the Pharisees,* and we must prepare an answer.

[23]John replied with the words of Isaiah:

**John the Immerser:** *Listen!* I am a voice calling out in the wilderness.

Straighten out the road for the Lord. *He's on His way.*[*]

[24-25]Then, some priests who were sent by the Pharisees started in on him again.

**Religious Leaders:** How can you *travel the countryside* cleansing[*] people for their sins if you are not the Liberator or Elijah or the Prophet?

**John the Immerser:** [26]Cleansing[*] with water is what I do, but the One *whom I speak of, whom we all await,* is standing among you and you have no idea who He is. [27]Though He comes after me, I am not even worthy to unlace His sandals.[*]

---

* 1:23 Isaiah 40:3
* 1:24-25 Literally, immersing, to show repentance
* 1:26 Literally, immersion, to show repentance
* 1:27 Verse 28 has been moved before verse 20 to retain the continuity of events.

*T*he mystery of Jesus' identity occupied us and will occupy generations of believers for centuries to come. As we journeyed with Him, it gradually became clearer who this man was, where He came from, and how His existence would profoundly affect the rest of human history. The question of "Who is this man?" was not answered overnight.

²⁹The morning after *this conversation as John is going about his business,* he sees *the Voice,* Jesus, coming toward him. *In eager astonishment* he shouts out:

**John the Immerser:** Look! *This man is more than He seems!* He is the Lamb sent from God, *the sacrifice* to erase the sins of the world! ³⁰He is the One I have been saying will come after me, who existed long before me and is much greater than I. ³¹*No one here* recognized Him—myself included. I came ritually cleansing* with water so that He might be revealed to Israel. ³²⁻³³And, just as the One who sent me told me, I knew who He was the moment I saw the Spirit come down upon Him as a dove and seal itself to Him. Now, He will cleanse* with the Holy Spirit. ³⁴I give my oath that everything I have seen is true. *If you don't believe now, keep listening.* He is *the Voice,* the Son of God!

³⁵⁻³⁶The day after, John *saw Him again as he* was visiting with two of his disciples. As Jesus walked by, he announced again:

**John the Immerser:** Do you see Him? This man is the Lamb of God; *He will be God's sacrifice to cleanse our sin.*

³⁷At that moment the two disciples began to follow Jesus, ³⁸⁻³⁹who turned back to them, saying:

**Jesus:** What is it that you want?

---

* 1:31 Literally, immersion, to show repentance
* 1:32-33 Literally, immerse

**Two Disciples:** We'd like to know where You are staying. Teacher, *may we remain at Your side today?*
**Jesus:** Come and see. *Follow Me, and we will camp together.*

It was about four o'clock in the afternoon *when they met Jesus.* They came and they saw where He was staying *but they got more than they imagined.* They remained with Him the rest of the day *and followed Him for the rest of their lives.* [40-41]One of these new disciples, Andrew, rushed to find his brother Simon and tell him they had found the Christ, the Liberating King, *the One who will heal the world.* [42]As Andrew approached with Simon, Jesus looked into him.

**Jesus:** Your name is Simon, and your father is called John. But from this day forward you will be known as Peter,[*] the rock.

[43-44]The next day Jesus set out to Galilee; and when He came upon Philip, He invited him to join them,

**Jesus:** Follow Me.

Philip, like Andrew and Peter, came from a town called Bethsaida *and he decided to make the journey with Him.* [45]Philip found Nathanael, *a friend, and burst in with excitement:*

**Philip:** We have found the One. Moses wrote about Him in the Law; all the prophets spoke of the day when He would come, and now He is here—His name is Jesus, son of Joseph *the carpenter*, and He comes from Nazareth.
**Nathanael:** [46]How can anything good come from *a place like* Nazareth?
**Philip:** Come with me. See *and hear* for yourself.

[47]As they approached, Jesus saw Nathanael coming.

**Jesus:** Look closely and you will see an Israelite who is a truth-teller.

---

[*] 1:42 Aramaic *Cephas*

**Nathanael:** [48]How would You know this about me? *We have never met.*

**Jesus:** *I have been watching you* before Philip invited you here. *Earlier in the day* you were enjoying *the shade and fruit of* the fig tree. I saw you then.

**Nathanael:** [49]Teacher, *I am sorry—forgive me.* You are the One—God's own Son and Israel's King.

**Jesus:** [50]Nathanael, if all it takes for you to believe is My telling you I saw you under the fig tree, then what you will see later shall astound you. *The miracles you will witness are greater than your imagination can comprehend.* [51]I tell you the truth: *before our journey is complete,* you will see the heavens standing open while heavenly messengers ascend and descend, *swirling* around the Son of Man.

*Chapter 2*

[1-2]Three days after *the disciples encountered Jesus for the first time,* they were all invited to celebrate a wedding feast in Cana of Galilee together with Mary, the mother of Jesus. [3]While they were celebrating, the wine ran out and Jesus' mother hurried over to her son.

**Mary:** *The host stands on the brink of embarrassment; there are many guests and* there is no more wine.

**Jesus:** [4]Dear woman, is it our problem *they miscalculated when buying wine and inviting guests*? My time has not arrived.

[5]*But Mary sensed the time was near. So in a way that only a mother can,* she turned to the servants.

**Mary:** Do whatever my son tells you.

⁶In that area were six *massive* stone water pots that could each hold 20 to 30 gallons.* They were typically used for Jewish purification rites. ⁷Jesus' instructions *were clear*:

**Jesus:** Fill each water pot with water until it's ready to spill over the top, ⁸then fill a cup and deliver it to the headwaiter.

They did exactly as they were instructed. ⁹After tasting the water that had become wine, the headwaiter couldn't figure out where such wine came from (even though the servants knew) and he called over the bridegroom *in amazement*.

**Headwaiter:** ¹⁰*This wine is delectable*. Why would you save the most exquisite fruit of the vine? A host would generally serve the good wine first and, when his inebriated guests don't notice or care, he would serve the inferior wine. You have held back the best for last.

¹¹Jesus performed this miracle, the first of His signs, in Cana of Galilee. *They did not know how this happened,* but when the disciples *and the servants* witnessed this miracle, their faith blossomed.

¹²Jesus then gathered His clan—His family members and disciples—for a journey to Capernaum where they lingered several days. ¹³The time was near to celebrate the Passover, *the festival commemorating when God rescued His children from slavery in Egypt*, so Jesus went to Jerusalem *for the celebration*. ¹⁴*Upon arriving*, He entered the temple *to worship and honor the Father. But it did not have the appearance of a holy place. The porches and colonnades* were filled with merchants selling *sacrificial animals, such as* doves, oxen, and sheep, and exchanging money. ¹⁵*In a display that can only be described as a righteous anger*, Jesus fashioned a whip of cords and used it *with skill* driving out animals; He scattered the money and overturned the tables, emptying profiteers from the house of God. ¹⁶There were dove merchants *still standing around*, and Jesus reprimanded them.

---

* 2:6 Greek *two to three metretes*

**Jesus:** *What are you still doing here?* Get all your stuff and haul it out of here! Stop making My Father's house a place for your own profit!

[17]*The disciples were astounded*, but they remembered that the Hebrew Scriptures said "jealous devotion for God's house consumes me."* [18] Some of the Jews cried out to Him *in unison.*

**Jews:** Who gave You the right to shut us down? *If it is God, then* show us a sign.
**Jesus:** [19]*You want a sign? Here it is.* Destroy this temple, and I will rebuild it in three days.
**Jews:** [20]*Three days?* This temple took more than 46 years to complete. You think You can replicate that feat in 3 days?

[21]*Jesus was planting seeds of truth in them.* The true temple was His body, *which would be destroyed on the cross and rebuilt in the resurrection.* [22]His disciples remembered this bold prediction after He was resurrected. *Because of this knowledge,* their faith in the Hebrew Scriptures and in Jesus' teachings grew.

    [23]During the Passover feast in Jerusalem *the crowds were watching Jesus closely*, and many began to believe in Him because of the signs He was doing. [24-25]But Jesus saw through to the heart of humankind, and He chose not to give them what they requested. He didn't need anyone to prove to Him the character of humanity. He knew what man was made of— *the dust of the earth—and they needed the seeds He was planting.*

---

* 2:17 Psalm 69:9

> *A*t this time our Roman occupiers had given a small group of Pharisees limited powers to rule, and Nicodemus was one of those Pharisees. He held a seat on the ruling council known as the Sanhedrin, and surprisingly Nicodemus was among those who sought out Jesus for His teaching. It appeared that he believed more about Jesus than he wanted others to know. So he came at night.

¹Nicodemus was one of the Pharisees, a man with some clout among his people. ²He came to Jesus under the cloak of darkness to question Him.

**Nicodemus:** Teacher, some of us have been talking. You are obviously a teacher who has come from God. The signs You are doing are proof that God is with You.

**Jesus:** ³I tell you the truth: only someone who experiences birth for a second time\* can *hope to* see the kingdom of God.

**Nicodemus:** ⁴*I am a grown man.* How can someone be born again when they are old *like me*? Am I to crawl back into my mother's womb for a second birth? *That's impossible!*

**Jesus:** ⁵I tell you the truth, if someone does not experience water and Spirit birth, there's no chance they will make it into God's kingdom. ⁶*Like from like.* Whatever is born from flesh is flesh; whatever is born from Spirit is spirit. ⁷Don't be shocked by My words, *but I tell you the truth.* Even you, *an educated and respected man among your people,* must be reborn *by the Spirit to enter the kingdom of God.* ⁸The wind\* blows all around us as if it has a will of its own; we *feel and* hear it, but we do not understand where it has come from

---

\* 3:3 Or "from above."
\* 3:8 "Wind" and "spirit" are the same word in Greek.

or where it will end up. Life in the Spirit is as if it were the wind of God.

**Nicodemus:** [9]I still do not understand how this can be.

**Jesus:** [10]Your responsibility is to instruct Israel *in matters of faith,* but you do not comprehend *the necessity of life in the Spirit?* [11]I tell you the truth: we speak about the things we know and we give evidence about the things we have seen, and you choose to reject *the truth of* our witness. [12]If you do not believe when I talk to you about ordinary, earthly realities, then heavenly realities will certainly elude you. [13]No one has ever journeyed to heaven above except the One who has come down from heaven—the Son of Man, who is of heaven. [14]Moses lifted up the serpent in the wilderness. In the same way, the Son of Man must be lifted up; [15]then all those who believe in Him will experience everlasting life.

[16]For God expressed His love for the world in this way: He gave His only Son so that whoever believes in Him will not face everlasting destruction, but will have everlasting life. [17]Here's the point. God didn't send His Son into the world to judge it; instead, He is here to rescue a world *headed toward certain destruction.*

[18]No one who believes in Him has to fear condemnation; yet condemnation is already the reality for everyone who refuses to believe. *Whoever embraces unbelief swims in a sea of judgment,* because he *chooses to ignore the Voice, and in doing so* rejects the name of the only Son of God. [19]Why does God allow for judgment *and condemnation?* Because the Light, *sent from God,* pierced through the world's darkness *to expose ill motives, hatred, gossip, greed, violence, and the like.* Still some people preferred the darkness over the light because their actions were dark. [20]Some of humankind hated the light *and so avoided its warm glow.* They *scampered hurriedly* back into the darkness where vices thrive and wickedness flourishes. [21]Those who *abandon deceit and* embrace what is true, they will enter into the light where it will be clear that all their deeds come from God.

> *J*esus made the point clear: stay connected to Him, and you will have no reason to fear. Jesus doesn't mean that the instant you have faith fear simply vanishes or only good things happen in your life. In fact, the blessings that come with eternal life often have nothing to do with present or future circumstances; but they have everything to do with our connections to God and one another. That is my message to all of you. God came to earth wrapped in flesh, and then He reached His greatest acclaim through a torturous death. If this is all true, then we will find strength and beauty in places we never imagined. Abiding in Jesus the Liberator is the good life, regardless of the external circumstances.

²²Not long after, Jesus and His disciples traveled to the Judean countryside where they could enjoy one another's company and ritually cleanse* *new followers*. ²³⁻²⁴About the same time, *Jesus' cousin* John—*the wandering prophet* who had not yet been imprisoned—*was upriver* at Aenon near Salim ritually cleansing* *scores of* people in the abundant waters there. ²⁵John's activities raised questions about the nature of purification among his followers and a religious leader, ²⁶so they approached him with their questions.

**John's Followers:** Teacher, the One who was with you *earlier* on the other side of the Jordan, the One whom you have been pointing to is ritually washing* the multitudes who are coming to Him.

**John the Immerser:** ²⁷Apart from the gifts that come from heaven, no one can receive anything at all. ²⁸I have said it many times, and you have heard me—I am not the Liberating King; I am the one who comes before Him. ²⁹If you are confused, consider this: the groom is the one with the bride. The best man takes his place close by and listens for him. When he hears the voice of the groom, he is swept

---

* 3:22 Literally, immersion, in an act of repentance
* 3:23-24 Literally, immersion, in an act of repentance
* 3:26 Literally, immersion, in an act of repentance

up in the joy *of the moment.* So hear me. My joy could not be more complete. ³⁰He, *the groom,* must take center stage, and I, *the best man,* must step to His side.

³¹If someone comes from heaven above, he ranks above it all *and speaks of heavenly things.* If someone comes from the earth, he speaks of earthly things. The One from the heavens is superior; He is over all. ³²He reveals the mysteries seen and *realities* heard *of the heavens above,* but no one below is listening. ³³Those who are listening and accept His witness *to these truths* have gone on record. They acknowledge the fact that God is true! ³⁴The One sent from God speaks with the very words of God and abounds with the very Spirit and essence of God. ³⁵The Father loves the Son and withholds nothing from Him. ³⁶Those who believe in the Son will bask in eternal life, but those who disobey the Son will never experience life. They will know only God's lingering wrath.

*Chapter 4*

¹⁻³The picture was becoming clear to the Pharisees that Jesus, whose disciples were busy ritually cleansing* many new disciples, had gained a following much larger than John, *the wandering prophet.* Because the Lord could see *that the Pharisees were beginning to plot against Him,* He chose to leave Judea *where most Pharisees lived* and return to *a safer location in* Galilee, ⁴a trip that would take them through Samaria.

> *F*or us, Samaria was a place to be avoided. Before Solomon's death 1,000 years earlier, the regions of Samaria and Judea were part of a united Israel. After the

---

* 4:1-3 Literally, immersion, in an act of repentance

rebellion that divided the kingdom, Samaria became a hotbed of idol worship. The northern kings made alliances that corrupted the people by introducing foreign customs and strange gods. They even had the nerve to build a temple to the true God on Mt. Gerizim to rival the one in Jerusalem. By the time we were traveling with Jesus, it was evident that the Samaritans had lost their way. By marrying outsiders, they had polluted the land. We considered them to be half-breeds—mongrels—and we knew we had to watch out for them or else we might be bitten.

5-8In a *small* Samaritan town known as Sychar, Jesus *and His entourage* stopped to rest at the historic well that Jacob gave his son Joseph. It was about noon when Jesus found a spot to sit close to the well while the disciples ventured off to find provisions. *From His vantage He watched as* a Samaritan woman approached to draw some water. *Unexpectedly,* He spoke to her.

**Jesus:** Would you *draw water and* give Me a drink.
**Woman:** 9I cannot believe that You, a Jew, would associate with me, a Samaritan woman, much less ask me to give You a drink.

Jews, you see, have no dealings with Samaritans. *Besides, a man would never approach a woman like this in public. Jesus was breaking accepted social barriers with this confrontation.*

**Jesus:** 10You don't know the gift of God or who is asking you for a drink *of this water from Jacob's well.* Because if you did, you would have asked Him *for something greater* and He would have given you the living water.
**Woman:** 11Sir, You sit by this deep well *a thirsty man* without a bucket in sight. Where does this living water come from? *Do You believe You can draw water and share it with me?* 12Are You claiming superiority to our father Jacob who labored long and hard to dig *and maintain* this well so that

he could share clean water with his sons, *grandchildren,* and cattle?

**Jesus:** [13]Drink this water, and your thirst is quenched only for a moment. *You must return to this well again and again.* [14]I offer water that will become a wellspring within you that gives life throughout eternity. You will never be thirsty again.

**Woman:** [15]*Please,* Sir, give me some of this water, so I'll never be thirsty and never again have to make the trip to this well.

**Jesus:** [16]Then bring your husband to Me.

**Woman:** [17-18]I do not have a husband.

**Jesus:** Technically you are telling the truth. But you have had five husbands and are currently living with a man you are not married to.

**Woman:** [19]Sir, it is obvious to me that You are a prophet. *Maybe You can explain to me why our peoples disagree about how to worship:* [20]Our fathers worshiped here on this mountain, but Your people say that Jerusalem is the only place for all to worship. *Which is it?*

**Jesus:** [21-24]Woman, I tell you that neither *is so.* Believe this: a new day is coming—in fact, it's already here—when the importance will not be placed on the time and place of worship but on the truthful hearts of worshipers. You worship what you don't know while we worship what we do know, for God's salvation is coming through the Jews. The Father is spirit, and He is seeking followers whose worship is sourced in truth and deeply spiritual as well. Regardless of whether you are in Jerusalem or on this mountain, if you do not seek the Father, then you do not worship.

**Woman:** [25]These mysteries will be made clear by the coming Liberator, the Anointed One.

---

*J*esus is often called "Christ." But "Christ" is not a name; it is the Greek translation of the Hebrew title "Messiah," which means in English "Liberating King." To call Jesus "the Christ" is to confess "Jesus is the Liberating King" or "the Anointed." The term "Liberating King" refers to a human being, God's end-time agent destined to bring universal peace and justice to our world. Jesus did just that when He spoke with the Samaritan woman. As the Liberating King, He could speak with her regardless of her heritage, lifestyle, or gender and offer her freedom from sin and peace.

**Jesus:** ²⁶The Liberating King speaks to you. I am the One you have been looking for.

²⁷The disciples returned to Him *and gathered around Him* in amazement that He would *openly break their customs by* speaking to this woman, but none of them would ask Him what He was looking for or why He was speaking with her. ²⁸The woman went back to the town, leaving her water pot behind. She stopped men *and women* on the streets and told them about what had happened.

**Woman:** ²⁹*I met* a stranger who knew everything about me. Come and see for yourselves; can He be the Liberating King?

³⁰A crowd came out of the city and approached Jesus. ³¹During all of this the disciples were urging Jesus to eat the food they gathered.

**Jesus:** ³²I have food to eat that you know nothing about.
**Disciples** (*to one another*): ³³Is it possible someone else has brought Him food while we were away?
**Jesus:** ³⁴I receive My nourishment by serving the will of the Father who sent Me and completing His work. ³⁵You have heard others say, "*Be patient;* we have four more months to wait until the crops are ready for the harvest." I say, take a closer look and you will see that the fields are ripe and ready for the harvest. ³⁶The harvester is collecting his pay, harvesting fruit ripe for eternal life. So even now he and the sower are celebrating *their fortune.* ³⁷The saying *may be old,*

*but it* is true: "One person sows, and another reaps." ³⁸I sent you to harvest where you have not labored; someone else took the time to plant and cultivate, and you feast on the fruit of their labor.

³⁹Meanwhile, because one woman shared with her neighbors how Jesus exposed her past and present, the village *of Sychar* was transformed—many Samaritans heard and believed. ⁴⁰The Samaritans approached Jesus and repeatedly invited Him to stay with them, so He lingered there for two days *on their account.* ⁴¹With the words that came from His mouth there were many more believing Samaritans. ⁴²They began their faith journey because of the testimony of the woman *beside the well,* but when they heard for themselves they were convinced the One they were hearing was and is the Savior sent to rescue the entire world.

⁴³⁻⁴⁵After two days *of teaching and conversation,* Jesus proceeded to Galilee, where His countrymen received Him *with familiar smiles. These old friends should have been the first to believe;* after all, they witnessed His miracle at the feast in Jerusalem. But Jesus understood and often quoted *the maxim:* "No one honors a hometown prophet." *It took outsiders like the Samaritans to recognize Him.*

⁴⁶⁻⁴⁷As Jesus traveled to Cana (the village in Galilee where He transformed the water into *fine* wine), He was met by a government official *at one o'clock in the afternoon.* This man heard *a rumor that* Jesus left Judea and was heading to Galilee; and he came *in desperation* begging for Jesus' help because his young son was near death. *He was fearful that unless* Jesus would go with him to Capernaum, his son would have no hope.

**Jesus** *(to the official)*: ⁴⁸*My word is not enough*; you only believe when you see miraculous signs.

**Official:** ⁴⁹Sir, this is my son; please come with me before he dies.

**Jesus** *(interrupting him)*: ⁵⁰Go home and *be with your son; you have My word that* he will live.

When he heard the voice of Jesus, faith took hold of him and he turned to go home. [51]Before he reached his village, his servants met him on the road celebrating his son's miraculous recovery.

**Servants** (*to the official*): *One moment your son was hunched over burning with fever; then suddenly every sign of illness was gone.*
**Official:** [52]What time did this happen?
**Servants:** Yesterday about one o'clock in the afternoon.

[53]At that moment, it dawned on the father the exact time that Jesus spoke the words "he will live." After that, he believed; and *when he told* his family *about his amazing encounter with the Liberating King,* they believed too. [54]This was the second sign-miracle Jesus performed when He came back to Galilee from Judea.

*Chapter 5*

[1]When these events were completed, Jesus led His followers to Jerusalem where they would celebrate a Jewish feast* together.

> *J*esus took our little group of disciples into one of the most miserable places I have ever seen. It was a series of pools where the crippled and diseased would gather hoping to be healed. The stench was unbearable, and no sane person would willingly march into an area littered with such wretched and diseased bodies. We knew what could happen, what they had could have easily

---

* 5:1 Perhaps Passover.

> rubbed off on us. That kind of impurity was frightening,
> but we followed Him as He approached a crippled man on
> his mat.

²⁻³In Jerusalem, they came upon a pool by the sheep gate surrounded by five covered porches. In Hebrew, this place is called Bethesda.

Crowds of people lined the area, lying around the porches. *As they walked among the crowds, it became clear that* all of these people were *disabled in some way;* some were blind, lame, paralyzed, or plagued by diseases [and they were waiting for the waters to move. ⁴From time to time, a heavenly messenger would come to stir the water in the pool. Whoever reached the water first and got in after it was agitated would be healed of his or her disease.]* ⁵⁻⁶In the crowd, Jesus noticed one particular man who had been living with his disability for 38 years. He knew this man had been waiting here a long time.

**Jesus** *(to the disabled man)*: Are you *here in this place* hoping to be healed?

**Disabled Man:** ⁷Kind Sir, I wait, *like all of these people,* for the waters to stir, *but I cannot walk. If I am to be healed in the waters,* someone must carry me into the pool. *So the answer to Your question is yes—but I cannot be healed here unless someone will help me.* Without a helping hand, someone else beats me to the water's edge each time it is stirred.

**Jesus:** ⁸Stand up, carry your mat, and walk.

⁹At the moment Jesus uttered these words, a healing energy coursed through the man and returned life to his limbs—he stood and walked *for the first time in 38 years.* But this was the Sabbath Day; *and any work, including carrying a mat, was prohibited on this day.*

---

* 5:4 Some ancient manuscripts omit the end of verse 3 and all of verse 4.

*Y*ou can't even begin to imagine this man's excitement. His entire life had been defined by his illness. Now he was free from it. Free from the pain and weakness. Free from the depression that gripped his soul. Free too from the shame he had always known. Now he did not just walk—he ran and celebrated with friends and family. Everyone was rejoicing with him, except for some of the Jewish leaders. Instead, they drilled him with questions as if they could disregard this miracle.

**Jewish Leaders** (*to the man who had been healed*): [10]Must you be reminded that it is the Sabbath? You are not allowed to carry your mat today!

**Formerly Disabled Man:** [11]The man who healed me gave me specific instructions to carry my mat and go.

**Jewish Leaders:** [12]Who is the man who gave you these instructions? *How can we identify Him?*

[13]The man genuinely did not know who it was that healed him. In the midst of the crowd *and the excitement of his renewed health,* Jesus had slipped away. [14]Some time later Jesus found him in the temple and again spoke to him.

**Jesus:** Take a look at your body; it has been made whole and strong. So avoid a life of sin or else a calamity greater than any disability may befall you.

[15]The man went immediately to tell the Jewish leaders that Jesus was the mysterious healer. [16]So they began pursuing and attacking Jesus because He performed these miracles on the Sabbath.

**Jesus** (*to His attackers*): [17]My Father is at work. So I too am working.

*T*his issue kept arising from the Jewish leaders. They did not appreciate the good things that Jesus did on the Sabbath. But Jesus was very clear about this. He cared for the poor, the sick, the marginalized more than He cared for how some people might interpret and apply God's law. You see, it is easy to turn law into a set of rules; it is much harder to care for the things of the heart. He also made it clear to us who followed His path—we were here to serve. Our service came out of love for our Liberator. All who followed Him were to love and to serve, especially on the Sabbath.

[18]*Most Jews cowered at the rebuke from these men, but Jesus did not. In fact,* He was justifying the importance of His work on the Sabbath, claiming God as His Father in ways that suggested He was equal to God. These pious religious leaders sought an opportunity to kill Jesus, and these words fueled their hatred.

**Jesus:** [19]The truth is that the Son does nothing on His own; *all these actions are led by the Father.* The Son watches the Father closely and then mimics the work of the Father. [20]The Father loves the Son, so He does not hide His actions. Instead, He shows Him everything, and the things not yet revealed by the Father will dumbfound you. [21]The Father can give life to those who are dead; in the same way, the Son can give the gift of life to those He chooses.

[22]The Father does not *exert His power to* judge anyone. Instead, He has given the authority as Judge to the Son. [23]So all of creation will honor *and worship* the Son as they do the Father. If you do not honor the Son, then you dishonor the Father who sent Him.

[24]I tell you the truth: eternal life belongs to those who hear My voice and believe in the One who sent Me. These people have no reason to fear judgment because they have already left death and entered life.

[25]I tell you the truth: a new day is imminent—in fact, it has arrived—when the voice of the Son of God will penetrate death's domain and everyone who hears will live. [26-27]You see, the Father radiates with life, and He also animates the Son *of God* with the same life-giving *beauty and* power to exercise judgment *over all of creation*. Indeed, the Son of God is also the Son of Man. [28]If this sounds amazing to you, what is even more amazing is that when the time comes, those buried long ago will hear His voice *through all the rocks, sod, and soil* [29]and step out *of decay into resurrection. When this hour arrives,* those who did good will be resurrected to life, and those who did evil will be resurrected to judgment.

[30]I have not ever, and will not in the future, act on My own. I listen *to the directions of the One who sent Me* and act *on these divine instructions. For this reason,* My judgment is always fair and never self-serving. I'm committed to pursuing God's agenda and not My own.

[31]If I stand as the lone witness to My true identity, then I can be dismissed as a liar. [32]*But if you listen,* you will hear another testify about Me and I know what He says about Me is genuine and true. [33]You sent *messengers* to John, and he told the truth *to everyone who would listen.* [34]Still his message about Me *originated in heaven* not in mortal man. I am telling you these things *for one reason*—so that you might be rescued. [35]*The voice of* John, *the wandering prophet,* is like a light in the darkness; and for a time, you took great joy and pleasure in the light he offered.

[36]There's another witness standing in My corner who is greater than John, *or any other man*. The mission that brings Me here, and the things I am called to do, demonstrate the authenticity of My calling, which comes directly from the Father. [37]In the act of sending Me, the Father has endorsed Me. *None of you knows the Father*. You have never heard His voice or seen His profile. [38]His word does not abide in you because you do not believe in the One sent by the Father.

[39]Here you are scouring through the Scriptures, hoping

that you will find eternal life among a pile of scrolls. *What you don't seem to understand is that* the Scriptures point to Me. [40]*Here I am with you,* and still you reject the truth *contained in the law and prophets* by refusing to come to Me so that you can have life. *I am the source of life, the animating energy of creation that you desperately lack.*

[41]This kind of glory does not come from mortal men. [42]*I stand before you with eyes that penetrate your soul,* and I see that you do not possess the love of God. [43]I have *pursued you*, coming here in My Father's name, and you have turned Me away. If someone else were to approach you with a different set of credentials, you would welcome him. [44]*That's why it is hard to see* how true faith is even possible for you: you are consumed by the approval of other men, *longing to look good in their eyes,* and yet you disregard the approval of the one true God. [45]Don't worry that I might bring you up on charges before My Father. Moses is your accuser even though you've put your hope in him; [46]because if you believed *what* Moses had to *say*, then you would believe in Me because he wrote about Me. [47]But if you ignore Moses and the deeper meaning of his writings, then how will you ever believe what I have to say?

## Chapter 6

[1]Once this had transpired, Jesus made His way to the other side of the Sea of Galilee (which some these days call the Sea of Tiberias). [2]As Jesus walked, a large crowd pursued Him hoping to see new signs *and miracles*; His healings of the sick and lame were garnering great attention. [3]Jesus went up a mountain and found a place to sit down *and teach*. His disciples gathered around. [4]The celebration of the Passover, one of

the principal Jewish feasts, would take place soon. [5]But when Jesus looked up, He could see an immense crowd coming toward Him. Jesus approached Philip.

**Jesus** *(to Philip)*: Where is a place to buy bread so these people may eat?

[6]Jesus knew what He was planning to do, but He asked Philip nonetheless. He had something to teach, and it started with a test.

**Philip:** [7]I could work for more than half of a year[*] and still not have the money to buy enough bread to give each person a very small piece.

[8]Andrew, the disciple who was Simon Peter's brother, spoke up.

**Andrew:** [9]I met a young boy in the crowd carrying five barley loaves and two fish, but that is practically useless in feeding a crowd this large.

**Jesus:** [10]Tell the people to sit down.

They all sat together on a large grassy area. *Those counting the people reported* approximately 5,000 men—*not counting the women and children*—sitting in the crowd. [11]Jesus picked up the bread, gave thanks to God, and passed it to everyone. He repeated this ritual with the fish. *Men, women, and children* all ate to their heart's content. [12]When the people had all they could eat, He told the disciples *to gather the leftovers.*

**Jesus:** Go and collect the leftovers, so we are not wasteful.

[13]They filled 12 baskets with fragments of the five barley loaves. [14]After witnessing this sign-miracle that Jesus did, the people stirred in conversation.

---

* 6:7 Greek *200 denarii*

**Crowd:** This man must be the Prophet *God said was* coming into the world.

[15]Jesus sensed the people were planning to mount a revolution *against Israel's Roman occupiers* and make Him king, so He withdrew further up the mountain by Himself.

> *Y*ou have to remember what we had experienced as a people. Since the Babylonians seized Judah in 586 B.C., we, the Jews, had one foreign occupier after another in our land. As conquerors go, the Romans weren't all that bad. They allowed us to worship God in His temple, and they appointed certain ones of us to govern. Of course, we still longed to rule ourselves and throw the Roman rulers out. Some of our people thought Jesus was just the man to lead that revolution. But political upheaval wasn't what He was teaching, and it wasn't why He came to earth.

[16]Later that evening the disciples walked down to the sea, [17]boarded a boat, and set sail toward Capernaum. Twilight gave way to darkness. Jesus had not yet joined them. [18]*Suddenly,* the waves rose and a fierce wind began *to rock the boat.* [19]After rowing three or four miles* *through the stormy seas,* they spotted Jesus approaching the boat walking mysteriously upon the deep waters that surrounded them. They panicked.

**Jesus** *(to the disciples)*: [20]I am the One. Don't be afraid.

[21]They welcomed Jesus aboard their small vessel; and when He stepped into the boat, the next thing they knew, they were ashore at their destination.
 [22]The following day some people gathered on the other side of the sea and saw that only one boat had been there; *they were perplexed.* They remembered seeing the disciples getting into the boat without Jesus, *but somehow Jesus was gone. How did He cross the sea without a boat?*

---

* 6:19 Greek *25 or 30 stadia*

²³Other boats were arriving from Tiberias near the grassy area where the Lord offered thanks and passed out bread. ²⁴When this crowd could not find Him or His disciples, they boarded their small boats and crossed the sea to Capernaum looking for Him. ²⁵When they found Jesus across the sea, they questioned Him.

Crowd: Teacher, when did You arrive at Capernaum?

Jesus: ²⁶I tell you the truth—you are tracking Me down because I fed you, not because you saw signs from God. ²⁷Don't spend your life chasing food that spoils and rots. Instead, seek the food that lasts into all the ages and comes from the Son of Man, the One on whom God the Father has placed His seal.

Crowd: ²⁸What do we have to do to accomplish the Father's works?

Jesus: ²⁹If you want to do God's work, then believe in the One He sent.

Crowd: ³⁰Can You show us a miraculous sign? *Something spectacular?* If we see something like that, it will help us to believe. ³¹Our fathers ate manna when they wandered in the desert. The Hebrew Scriptures say, "He gave them bread from heaven to eat."*

Jesus: ³²I tell you the truth, Moses did not give you bread from heaven; it is My Father who offers you true bread from heaven. ³³The bread of God comes down out of heaven and breathes life into the cosmos.

Crowd: ³⁴Master, we want a boundless supply of this bread.

Jesus: ³⁵I am the bread that gives life. If you come to My table and eat, you will never go hungry. Believe in Me, and you will never go thirsty. ³⁶Here I am standing in front of you, and still you don't believe. ³⁷All that My Father gives to Me comes to Me. I will receive everyone; I will not send away anyone who comes to Me. ³⁸And here's the reason: I have come down from heaven not to pursue My own agenda but to do what He desires. I am here on behalf of the Father who sent Me. ³⁹He sent Me to care for all He has given Me,

---

* 6:31 Exodus 16:4

so that nothing *and no one* will perish. *In the end,* on the last day He wants everything to be resurrected *into new life.* ⁴⁰So if you want to know the will of the Father, know this: everyone who sees the Son and believes in Him will live eternally, and on the last day I am the One who will resurrect him.

⁴¹Some of the Jews began to *quietly* grumble against Him because He said "I am the bread that came down from heaven." *Wasn't He a human just like everyone else?*

**Crowd:** ⁴²Isn't Jesus the son of Joseph? We know His parents! *We know where He came from,* so how can He claim to have "come down from heaven"?

**Jesus:** ⁴³Stop grumbling *under your breaths.* ⁴⁴If the Father who sent Me does not draw you, then there's no way you can come to Me. But I will resurrect everyone who does come on the last day. ⁴⁵Among the prophets it's written, "Everyone will be taught of God."* So everyone who has heard and learned from the Father finds Me. ⁴⁶No one has seen the Father, except the One sent from God. He has seen the Father. ⁴⁷I am telling you the truth: the one who accepts these things has eternal life. ⁴⁸I am the life-bread. ⁴⁹Your fathers ate manna in the wilderness, and they died *as you know.* ⁵⁰But there is another bread that comes from heaven; if you eat this bread, you will not die. ⁵¹I am the living bread that has come down from heaven *to rescue those who eat it.* Anyone who eats this bread will live forever. The bread that I will give breathes life into the cosmos. This bread is My flesh.

⁵²*The low whispers of* some of Jesus' detractors turned into an out-and-out debate.

**Crowd:** *What is He talking about?* How is He able to give us His flesh to eat?

---

* 6:45 Isaiah 54:13

**Jesus:** [53]I tell you the truth; unless you eat the flesh of the Son of Man and drink His blood, you will not know life. [54]If you eat My flesh and drink My blood, then you will have eternal life, and I will raise you up at the end of time. [55]My flesh and blood provide true nourishment. [56]If you eat My flesh and drink My blood, you will abide in Me and I will abide in you. [57]The Father of life who sent Me has given life to Me; and as you eat My flesh, I will give life to you. [58]This is bread that came down from heaven; I am not like the manna that your fathers ate and then died! If you eat this bread, your life will never end.

*H*ow is it that we can follow this path and believe these truths? To be honest, it is not easy. In fact, some found this so hard that they left Jesus for good. The rest of us would readily admit that we're still working on what it means to follow Him. So Jesus left behind a number of practices to help us. One of these is known as the Lord's Supper. Jesus instructed us to break bread and share wine to remember how He allowed His body to be broken for all humankind. In some beautiful, mysterious way, Jesus is present for us in the simple elements of bread and wine. Touch Him; taste His richness; remember His most glorious hour on the cross. In that moment, He embraced all darkness and shame and transformed them into light. As I come to the table with my community and we feast on His light, life seems more hopeful and complete. As you take the bread and the wine, you affirm the reality that the Liberating King is among and within you.

[59]He spoke these words in the synagogue as part of His teaching mission in Capernaum. [60]Many disciples heard what He said, and they had questions *of their own.*

**Disciples:** How are we supposed to understand all of this? It is a hard teaching.

[61]Jesus was aware that even His disciples were murmuring about this.

**Jesus:** Has My teaching offended you? [62]What if you were to see the Son of Man ascend *to return* to where He came from? [63]The Spirit brings life. The flesh has nothing to offer. The words I have been teaching you are spirit and life. [64]But some of you do not believe.

From the first day *Jesus began to call disciples,* He knew those who did not have genuine faith. He knew too who would betray Him.

**Jesus:** [65]This is why I have been telling you that no one comes to Me without the Father's blessing and guidance.

[66]After hearing these teachings, many of His disciples walked away and no longer followed Jesus.

**Jesus** *(to the twelve)*: [67]Do you want to walk away too?
**Simon Peter:** [68]Lord, if we were to go, who would we follow? You speak the words that give everlasting life. [69]We believe and recognize You as the Holy One of God.
**Jesus:** [70]I chose each one of you, the twelve, Myself. But one of you is a devil.

[71]This cryptic comment referred to Judas the son of Simon Iscariot, for he was the one of the twelve who was going to betray Him.

*Chapter 7*

[1]After these events, *it was time for Jesus to move on.* He began a long walk through the Galilean countryside. He was purposefully avoiding Judea because of *the violent threats made*

*against Him by* the Jews there who wanted to kill Him. *²It was fall,* the time of year when the Jews celebrated the Festival of Booths.

> *W*e always looked forward to this week-long festival filled with food, worship, prayer, and celebration. On this holiday, everyone moved out of their homes and camped in temporary quarters, called booths, to remember that God was with us as our ancestors wandered for 40 years without a home. It was common for us to celebrate these holidays with family, so the brothers of Jesus were with us as we discussed our destination. Where would we celebrate?

**Brothers of Jesus** (*to Jesus*): ³Let's get out of here and go *south* to Judea so You can show Your disciples there what You are capable of doing. ⁴No one who seeks the public eye is content to work in secret. If You want to perform these signs, then step forward on the world's stage; *don't hide up here in the hills, Jesus.*

⁵Jesus' own brothers *were speaking contemptuously;* they did not yet believe in Him, *just as the people in His hometown did not see Him as anything more than Joseph's son.*

**Jesus:** ⁶My time has not yet arrived, but for you My brothers, *by all means,* it is always the right time. *⁷You have nothing to worry about because the* world doesn't hate you, but it despises Me because I am always exposing the dark evil in its works. ⁸Go on to the feast without Me; I am not going *right now* because My time is not yet at hand.

⁹This conversation came to an *abrupt* end, and Jesus stayed in Galilee ¹⁰until His brothers were gone. Then He too went up to Jerusalem. But He traveled in secret to avoid drawing any public attention. ¹¹Some Jewish leaders were searching for Him at the feast and asking the crowds where they could find

Him. [12]The crowds would talk in groups: some favored Jesus and thought He was a good man; others disliked Him and thought He was leading people astray. [13]*All of these conversations took place in whispers.* No one was willing to speak openly about Jesus for fear of the religious leaders.

[14]In the middle of the festival, Jesus marched directly into the temple and started to teach. [15]Some of the Jews *who heard Him* were amazed at Jesus' ability, and people questioned repeatedly:

**Jews:** How can this man be so wise *about the Hebrew Scriptures*? He has never had a formal education.

**Jesus:** [16]I do not claim ownership of My words; they are *a gift* from the One who sent Me. [17]If anyone is willing to act according to His purposes *and is open to hearing truth*, he will know the source of My teaching. Does it come from God or from Me? [18]If a man speaks his own words, *constantly quoting himself*, he is after adulation. But I chase only after glory for the One who sent Me. My intention is *authentic and* true. You'll find no wrong *motives* in Me.

[19]Moses gave you the law, didn't he? Then how can you *blatantly* ignore the law and look for an opportunity to murder Me?

---

*N*otice how Jesus changed in tone and subject. This shift seemed abrupt to us because we didn't know anything about the Pharisees' plotting.

---

**Crowd:** [20]You must be possessed with a demon! Who is trying to kill You?

**Jesus:** [21]*Listen,* all it took was for Me to do one thing, *heal a crippled man,* and you all were astonished. [22]Don't you remember how Moses passed down circumcision as a tradition of our ancestors? When you pick up a knife to circumcise on the Sabbath, *isn't that work*? [23]If a male is circumcised on the Sabbath to keep the law of Moses intact, how can making one man whole on the Sabbath be a cause for your violent rage? <sup>24</sup>You should not judge by outward appearance. When you judge, search for what is right and just.

**Some People of Jerusalem:** <sup>25</sup>There is the man they are seeking to kill; surely He must be the one. <sup>26</sup>But here He is, speaking out in the open to the crowd, while they have not spoken a word to *stop or challenge* Him. *Do you think they've changed their minds?* Do these leaders now believe He is the Liberating King? <sup>27</sup>But He can't be; we know where this man comes from, but the true origin of the Liberator will be a mystery to all of us.

**Jesus** (*speaking aloud as He teaches on the temple's porch*): <sup>28</sup>*You think* you know Me and where I have come from, but I have not come here on My own. I have been sent by the One who embodies truth. You do not know Him. <sup>29</sup>I know Him because I came from Him. He has sent Me.

<sup>30</sup>Some were trying to seize Him because of His words, but no one laid as much as a finger on Him—His time had not yet arrived. <sup>31</sup>In the crowd, there were many in whom faith was taking hold.

**Believers in the Crowd:** When the Liberator arrives, will He perform any more signs than this man has done?

<sup>32</sup>Some Pharisees *were hanging back in the crowd*, overhearing the gossip about Him. The temple authorities and the Pharisees *took action and* sent officers to arrest Jesus.

**Jesus:** <sup>33</sup>I am going to be with you for a little while longer; then I will return to the One who sent Me. <sup>34</sup>You will look for Me, but you will not be able to find Me. Where I am, you are unable to come.

**Some Jews in the Crowd** (*to each other*): <sup>35</sup>Where could He possibly go that we could not find Him? You don't think He's about to go into the Dispersion<sup>*</sup> and teach our people scat-

---

<sup>*</sup> 7:35 Literally, the Diaspora (Greek for "scattering"). The Diaspora refers to those Jews who were exiled or settled outside the traditional lands of Israel.

tered among the Greeks, do you? [36]What do you think He means, "You will look for Me, but not be able to find Me," and "Where I am, you are not able to come"?

[37]On the last day, the biggest day of the festival, Jesus stood again and spoke aloud.

**Jesus:** If any of you is thirsty, come to Me and drink. [38]If you believe in Me, the Hebrew Scriptures say that rivers of living water will flow from within you.*

[39]Jesus was referring to *the realities of life in* the Spirit made available to everyone who believes in Him. But the Spirit had not yet arrived because Jesus had not been glorified.

*T*he Holy Spirit connects us to the Father and His Son, the Liberating King. So lay down any fear you have about being disconnected from God; the Creator of the Universe dwells within you, sustains you, and will accomplish the impossible through you.

After Jesus' exit, we, the church, take on our most important role as we become His body here on earth. We are intimately connected to the living God individually, but it also is important to remember our journey is to be shared in community.

The church is a redeeming force in the world: His hands, His feet, His body. If you want to know the Liberator, then you must know His body. Life in Him is not just about embracing and loving God; it's about being the living body of the church. We will find strength, passion, and comfort in our collective mission.

**Some of the Crowd** (*speaking aloud as He teaches on the temple's porch*): [40]This man is definitely the Prophet.
**Others:** [41]This is the Liberating King!

---

* 7:38 For example, Isaiah 44:3; 55:1; 58:11.

**Still Others:** Is it possible for the Liberator to come from Galilee? [42]Don't the Hebrew Scriptures say that He will come from Bethlehem,[*] King David's village, and be a descendant of King David?

[43]*Rumors and* opinions about the true identity of Jesus divided the crowd. [44]Some wanted to arrest Him, but no one dared to touch Him.

[45]The officers *who had been sent by* the chief priests and Pharisees *to take Jesus into custody* returned *empty-handed,* and they faced some hard questions.

**Chief Priest and Pharisees:** *Where is Jesus?* Why didn't you capture Him?

**Officers:** [46]*We listened to Him.* Never has a man spoken like this man.

**Pharisees:** [47]So you have also been led astray? [48]Can you find one leader or educated Pharisee who believes this man? *Of course not. Anyone who has studied the Scriptures knows His words are wrong and a threat to our people.* [49]This crowd is plagued by ignorance about the teachings of the law; *that is why they will listen to Him.* That is also why they are under God's curse.

[50]Nicodemus, *the Pharisee* who approached Jesus *under the cloak of darkness*, was present when the officers returned empty-handed. He addressed the leaders.

**Nicodemus:** [51]Does our law condemn someone without first giving him a fair hearing and learning something about him?

**Pharisees** *(ignoring Nicodemus's legal point)*: [52]Are you from Galilee too? Look it up for yourself; no real prophet is supposed to come from Galilee.

[53][The time came for everyone to go home.[*]

---

* 7:42 For example, Micah 5:1-2
* 7:53 The episode recorded in John 7:53—8:11 is not contained in many ancient manuscripts.

## Chapter 8

¹Jesus went to the Mount of Olives. ²He awoke early in the morning to return to the temple. *When He arrived,* the people surrounded Him, so He sat down and began to teach them. ³*While He was teaching,* the scribes and Pharisees brought in a woman who was caught in the act of adultery, and stood her before Jesus.

**Pharisees:** ⁴Teacher,

> *I*magine the tension in that moment. You can sense the sarcasm in the air as these men threatening Jesus are now calling Him "Teacher." Jesus knew this was a test.

**Pharisees:** This woman was caught in the act of adultery. ⁵Moses says in the law that we are to kill such women by stoning. What do You say about it?

⁶This was all set up as a test for Jesus; His answers would give them grounds to accuse Him *of crimes against Moses' law.* Jesus bent over and wrote something in the dirt with His finger. ⁷They persisted in badgering Jesus, so He stood up straight.

**Jesus:** Let the first stone be thrown by the one among you who has not sinned.

⁸Once again Jesus bent down to the ground and resumed writing with His finger. ⁹The Pharisees who heard Him *stood still for a few moments and then* began to leave slowly, one by one, beginning with the older men. *Even the pious Pharisees knew they had sinned, so there would be no stones thrown this day.* Eventually, only Jesus and the woman remained, ¹⁰and Jesus looked up.

**Jesus:** *Dear* woman, where is everyone? *Are we alone?* Did no one step forward to condemn you?
**Woman Caught in Adultery:** ¹¹Lord, no one *has condemned me.*
**Jesus:** Well, I do not condemn you either; *all I ask is that you* go and from now on avoid the sins that plague you.]*

¹²*On another occasion,* Jesus spoke to the crowds again.

**Jesus:** I am the light that shines through the cosmos; if you walk with Me, you will thrive in the *nourishing* light that gives life and will not know darkness.
**Pharisees:** ¹³Jesus, what You are claiming about Yourself cannot possibly be true. The only person bearing witness is You.
**Jesus:** ¹⁴Even if I am making *bold* claims about Myself—*who I am, what I have come to do*—I am speaking the truth. You see, I know where I came from and where I will go *when I am done here.* You know neither where I come from nor where I will go. ¹⁵You spend your time judging *by the wrong criteria,* by human standards, but I am not here to judge anyone. ¹⁶If I were to judge, then My judgment would be based on truth, but I would not judge anyone alone. I act in harmony with the One who sent Me. ¹⁷Your law states that if the testimonies of two witnesses agree, their testimony is true. ¹⁸Well, I testify about Myself, and so does the Father who sent Me here.
**Pharisees:** ¹⁹Where is the Father *who testifies on Your behalf?*
**Jesus:** You don't know the Father or Me. If you knew Me, then you would also know the Father.

²⁰Jesus said all of these things in the treasury while He was teaching in the temple; *followers and opponents alike gathered to hear Him,* but none of His enemies tried to seize Him because His time had not yet come.

**Jesus** *(to the crowds)*: ²¹I am leaving this place, and you will look for Me and die in your sin. For where I am going, you are not able to come.

---

* 7:53–8:11 Many ancient manuscripts omit these verses.

**Jews:** [22]Is He suicidal? He keeps saying, "Where I am going, you are not able to come." *Surely He does not have plans to kill Himself.*

**Jesus:** [23]You originate from *the earth* below, and I have come from *the heavens* above. You are from this world, and I am not. [24]That's why I told you that you will die here as a result of your sins. Unless you believe I am who I have said I am, your sins will lead to your death.

**Jews:** [25]Who exactly are You?

**Jesus:** From the beginning of My mission I have been telling you who I am. [26]I have so much to say about you, so many judgments to render, *but if you hear one thing,* hear that the One who sent Me is true, and all the things I have heard from Him I speak into the world.

[27]The people had not understood that Jesus was teaching about the Father.

**Jesus:** [28]Whenever *the day comes and* you lift up the Son of Man, then you will know that I am He. *It will be clear then* that I am not acting alone, but that I am speaking the things I have learned directly from the Father. [29]The One who sent Me is with Me; He has not abandoned Me because I always do what pleases Him.

[30]As Jesus was speaking, many in the crowd believed in Him. *But they could not imagine what He meant about the lifting up of the Son of Man.*

**Jesus** *(to the new Jewish believers)*: [31]If you *hear My voice* and abide in My word, you are truly My disciples; [32]and you will know the truth, and that truth will give you freedom.

**Jewish Believers:** [33]We are Abraham's children, and we have never been enslaved to anyone. How can You say to us, "You will be set free"?

**Jesus:** [34]I tell you the truth: everyone who commits sin surrenders his freedom to sin. *He is a slave to sin's power.* [35]Even a household slave does not live in the home like a member of the family, but a son belongs there forever. [36]So *think of it this way,* if the Son comes to make you free, you will really be free.

*Jesus noticed that some of His opponents were listening, so He spoke louder and turned His remarks to them.*

**Jesus:** [37]I know you are descendants of Abraham, but here you are plotting to murder Me. *You want Me dead, and for what reason?* Because you do not welcome My voice into your lives. [38]As I speak, I am painting you a picture of what I have seen with My Father; here you are repeating the things you have seen from your father.

**Jews:** [39]Abraham is our father.

**Jesus:** If you are truly Abraham's children, then act like Abraham! [40]From what I see you are trying to kill Me, a man who has told you the truth that comes from the Father. This is not something Abraham would do, [41]but you are doing what you have learned from your father.

**Jews:** We were not born from adulterous parents; we have one Father: God.

**Jesus:** [42]I come from the one true God, and I'm not here on My own. He sent Me *on a mission.* If God were your Father, you would *know that and* you would love Me. [43]You don't even understand what I'm saying. *Do you?* Why? It is because You cannot stand to hear My voice. [44]You are just like your true father, the devil, and you spend your time pursuing the things your father loves. He started out as a killer, and he cannot tolerate truth because he is void of anything true. At the core of his character, he is a liar; and everything he speaks originates in these lies because he is the father of lies. [45]So when I speak truth, you don't believe Me. [46-47]If I speak the truth, why don't you believe Me? If you belong to God's family, then why can't you hear God speak? The answer is clear; you are not in God's family. *I speak truth, and you don't believe Me.* Can any of you convict Me of sin?

**Jews:** [48]We were right when we called You a demon-possessed Samaritan.

**Jesus:** [49-50]I'm not taken by demons. You dishonor Me, but I give *all glory and* honor to the Father. But I am not pursuing My own fame. There is only One who pursues and renders justice. [51]I tell you the truth, anyone who *hears My voice and* keeps My word will never experience death.

**Jews:** [52]We are even more confident now that You are demon-possessed. *Just go down the list:* Abraham died, the prophets all died. Yet You say, "If you keep My word, you won't taste death." [53]Are you greater than our father Abraham? He died; *remember?* Prophets—are any of them still alive? No. Who do You think You are?

**Jesus:** [54]If I were trying to make Myself somebody important, *it would be a waste of time.* That kind of fame is worth nothing. It is the Father who *is behind Me, urging Me on,* giving Me praise. You say, "He is our God," [55]but you are not in relationship with Him. I know Him *intimately;* even if I said anything other than the truth, I would be a liar, like you. I know Him, and I do as He says. [56]Your father Abraham anticipated the time when I would come, and he celebrated My coming.

**Jews:** [57]You aren't even 50 years old, yet You have seen *and talked with* Abraham?

**Jesus:** [58]I tell you the truth; I AM before Abraham was born.

[59]The people picked up stones to hurl at Him, but Jesus slipped out of the temple. *Their murderous rage would have to wait.*

---

*I* have had a few things to say about "the Jews." You all seem to cringe every time the subject arises. People are overly sensitive about that. The fact is: I am a Jew. I am a son of Abraham, as are many in my community, so when I criticize certain Jewish leaders I am not criticizing a whole people. I'm not stereotyping or making generalizations. When I use the term "the Jews," I am talking about a corrupt group of power brokers who conspired against Jesus with the Romans to have Him crucified and who later had my people expelled from the synagogue. They are members of my family, and I can't stand what they did to Jesus and what they are doing to my other family, my faith family. Don't you remember the prophets? Men like Micah, Isaiah, and Amos? Prophets have the duty—Jeremiah said he had "a fire in his bones"[2]—to speak for God and condemn hypocrisy and unbelief wherever it is found. When injustice and unbelief are found close to home, prophets must speak. That's my call. That's what I'm doing.

## Chapter 9

[1]While walking *together* along the road, Jesus saw a man who was blind since his birth.

**Disciples:** [2]Teacher, who sinned? *Who is responsible for this man's blindness?* Did he commit sins that merited this punishment? If not his sins, is it the sins of his parents?

**Jesus:** [3]Neither. His blindness cannot be *explained or* traced to any particular person's sins. He is blind so the deeds of God may be put on display. [4]While it is daytime, we must do the works of the One who sent Me. But when the *sun sets and* night falls, this work is impossible. [5]Whenever I am in the world, I am the light of the world.

Certainly Jesus knew the Pharisees frowned on His Sabbath healings, but their opinions were not His motivation to finish before sunset. Jesus used the sunset

---

[2] Jeremiah 20:9

to make a point to us: just as the sun illuminates the world, He brings enlightenment; just as the sun is up for a short time each day, His time on earth is short.

[6]After He said these things, He spat on the ground and mixed saliva and dirt to form mud, which He smeared across the blind man's eyes.

**Jesus** (*to the blind man*): [7]Go, wash yourself in the pool of Siloam.

Siloam means "sent," *and its name reminded us that his healing was sent by God.* The man went, washed, and returned to Jesus, his eyes now alive with sight. [8]Then neighbors and others who knew him were confused to see a man so closely resembling the blind beggar running about.

**Townspeople:** Isn't this the man we see *every day* sitting and begging *in the streets*?
**Others:** [9]This is the same man.
**Still Others:** This cannot be him. But this fellow bears an uncanny resemblance to the blind man.
**Formerly Blind Man:** I am the same man. *It's me!*
**Townspeople:** [10]How have your *lifeless* eyes been opened?
**Formerly Blind Man:** [11]A man named Jesus *approached me and made mud* from the ground and applied it to my eyes. He then said to me, "Go, wash yourself in the pool of Siloam." I went and washed, and suddenly I could see.
**Townspeople:** [12]Where is this man *who healed you*?
**Formerly Blind Man:** I don't know.

[13-14]The townspeople brought the formerly blind beggar to appear before the Pharisees *the same day Jesus healed him,* which happened to be on the Sabbath Day. [15]The Pharisees began questioning him, looking for some explanation for how he could now see.

**Formerly Blind Man:** He smeared mud on my eyes, and I washed; now I see.

**Some Pharisees:** [16]God can't possibly be behind this man because He is breaking the rules of the Sabbath.

**Other Pharisees:** How can such a lawbreaking scoundrel do something like this?

The Pharisees were at odds with one another about Jesus and could not agree *whether His power came from God or the devil.*

**Pharisees** *(to the formerly blind man)*: [17]What do you say about this man, about the fact He opened your eyes so you could see?

**Formerly Blind Man:** *I have no doubt*—this man is a prophet.

[18]Some of the Jews suspected the whole situation was a charade, that this man was never blind. So they summoned the man's parents to testify about his condition.

**Pharisees:** [19]Is this man your son? Do you testify that he has been blind from birth? How therefore does he now see?

**Parents:** [20]We can tell you this much: he is our son, and he was born blind. [21]But his new sight is a complete mystery to us! We do not know the man who opened his eyes. Why don't you ask our son? He is old enough to speak for himself.

[22]The man's parents were a bit evasive because they were afraid of the Jewish leaders. It had been rumored that anyone who spoke of Jesus as the Liberating King would be expelled from the synagogue. [23]So they deferred the thorny question to their son, [24]and the Pharisees called on him a second time.

**Pharisees:** Give God the credit. *He's the One who healed you.* All glory belongs to God. We are persuaded this man you speak of is a sinner *who defies God.*

**Formerly Blind Man:** [25]If this man is a sinner, I don't know. *I am not qualified to say.* I only know one thing: I was blind and now I see.

**Pharisees:** [26]What did He do to you? How did He give you sight?

**Formerly Blind Man:** [27]*Listen,* I've already answered all these questions and you don't like my answers. Do you really need me to say it all over again? Are you thinking about joining up with Him and becoming His followers?

**Pharisees** *(berating him):* [28]You're one of His followers, but we follow Moses. [29]We have confidence that God spoke to Moses, but this man *you speak of is a mystery;* we don't even know where He comes from.

**Formerly Blind Man:** [30]Isn't it ironic that you, *our religious leaders,* don't even know where He comes from; yet He gave me sight! [31]We know that God does not listen to sinners, but He does respond and work through those who worship Him and do His will. [32]No one has ever heard of someone opening the eyes of any person blind from birth. [33]This man must come from God; otherwise, this miracle would not be possible. *Only God can do such things.*

**Pharisees:** [34]You were born under a cloud of sin. How can you, *of all people,* lecture us?

The religious leaders banished him from their presence. [35]Jesus heard what had happened and sought out the man.

**Jesus:** Do you believe in the Son of Man?

**Formerly Blind Man:** [36]I want to believe, Lord. Who is He?

**Jesus:** [37]You have seen His face *with your new eyes,* and you are talking to Him now.

**Formerly Blind Man:** [38]Lord, I do believe.

The man bowed low to worship Jesus.

**Jesus:** [39]I have entered this world to announce a verdict *that changes everything.* Now those without sight may begin to see, and those who see may become blind.

**Some Pharisees** *(who overheard Jesus):* [40]Surely we are not blind, are we?

**Jesus:** [41]If you were blind, you would be without sin. But because you claim you can see, your sin is ever present.

*I*t seemed like the Pharisees were frequently around to challenge whatever Jesus would say and do. But He would always get the better of them. Once again, Jesus turned what the Pharisees said inside out. They thought blindness was a curse that evidenced sin, and they thought vision ensured knowledge and understanding—even concerning spiritual matters. Instead, the Pharisees' confidence in their vision and discernment made them unable to see the truth about Jesus. Ironically, they had a blind trust in their sighted leaders. By refusing to believe in Him, they were the sinners—not the blind man.

## *Chapter 10*

**Jesus:** [1]I tell you the truth: the man who crawls though the fence of the sheep pen, rather than walking through the gate, is a thief or a vandal. [2]The shepherd walks openly through the entrance. [3]The guard who is posted to protect the sheep opens the gate for the shepherd, and the sheep hear his voice. He calls his own sheep by name and leads them out. [4]When all the sheep have been gathered, he walks on ahead of them, and they follow him because they know his voice. [5]The sheep would not be willing to follow a stranger; they run because they do not know the voice of strangers. *But they know and follow the shepherd's voice.*

[6]Jesus explained a profound truth through this metaphor, but they did not understand His teaching. [7]So He explained further.

**Jesus:** I tell you the truth: I am the gate of the sheep. [8]All who approached the sheep before Me came as thieves and robbers, and the sheep did not listen to their voices. ⁹I am the gate; whoever enters through Me will be liberated, will go in and go out, and will find pastures. ¹⁰The thief approaches *with malicious intent*, looking to steal, slaughter, and destroy; I came to give life with joy and abundance.

¹¹I am the good shepherd. The good shepherd lays down His life for the sheep *in His care*. ¹²The hired hand is not like the shepherd caring for His own sheep. When a wolf attacks, snatching and scattering the sheep, he runs for his life, leaving them *defenseless*. ¹³The hired hand runs because he works only for wages and does not care for the sheep. ¹⁴I am the good shepherd; I know My sheep, and My sheep know Me. ¹⁵As the Father knows Me, I know the Father; I will give My life for the sheep. ¹⁶There are many more sheep than you can see here, and I will bring them as well. They will hear My voice, and the flock will be united. One flock. One shepherd. ¹⁷The Father loves Me because I *am willing to* lay down My life—but I will take it up again. ¹⁸My life cannot be taken away by anybody else; I am giving it of My own free will. My authority allows Me to give My life and to take it again. All this has been commanded by My Father.

*J*esus loved to explain truth through the everyday things we encountered. He spoke of vines, fruit, fishing, building, and shepherding. He was a master communicator. In this metaphor, Jesus is the shepherd. Eventually, He would become the sheep as well. On the cross He was destined to become the innocent sacrifice that would make all future sin sacrifices and burnt offerings unnecessary.

¹⁹When He spoke these words, some of the Jews began to argue.

**Many Jews:** ²⁰He has a demon and is a raving maniac. Why are you people listening to Him?

**Other Jews:** ²¹No demon-possessed man ever spoke like this. Do demons give sight to the blind?

²²⁻²³It was winter and time for the Festival of Dedication.* While in Jerusalem, Jesus was walking through the temple in an area known as Solomon's porch, ²⁴and Jews gathered around Him.

**Jews:** How long are You going to keep us guessing? If You are the Liberating King, announce it clearly.

**Jesus:** ²⁵I have told you, and you do not believe. The works I am doing in My Father's name tell the truth about Me. *You do not listen;* ²⁶you lack faith because you are not My sheep. ²⁷My sheep *respond as they* hear My voice; I know them *intimately*, and they follow Me. ²⁸I give them a life that is unceasing, and death will not have the last word. *Nothing or* no one can steal them from My hand. ²⁹My Father has given the flock to Me, and He is superior to all *beings and things*. No one is powerful enough to snatch the flock from My Father's hand. ³⁰I and the Father are one.

³¹The Jews gathered stones to execute Jesus right then and there.

**Jesus:** ³²I have performed many beautiful works before you in the name of the Father. Which of these can be judged as an offense that merits My execution?

**Jews:** ³³You are not condemned for performing miracles. We demand Your life because You are a man, yet you claim to be God. This is blasphemy!

**Jesus:** ³⁴*You know* what is written in the Scriptures. Doesn't it read, "I said, you are gods"?* ³⁵If the Scriptures called your ancestors (*mere mortals*) gods to whom the word of God came—and the Scriptures cannot be set aside—³⁶what should you call One *who is unique*, sanctified by and sent from the Father into the world? I have said, "I am God's Son." How can you call that blasphemy? ³⁷*By all means,* do not believe in Me, if I am not doing the things of the Father. ³⁸But examine My actions, *and you will see that My work is*

---

* 10:22-23 Or the Festival of Lights or Hanukkah.
*10:34 Psalm 82:6

*the work of the Father.* Regardless of whether you believe in Me—believe the miracles. Then you will know that the Father is in Me, and I am in the Father.

³⁹Once again, *some of* the Jews again tried to capture Him; but He slipped away, eluding their grasp. ⁴⁰Jesus crossed the Jordan River and returned to the place where John was ritually cleansing* the people in the early days. He lingered in the area, ⁴¹and scores of people gathered around Him.

**Crowds:** John never performed any miracles, but every word he spoke about this man has come to pass. It is all true!

⁴²In that place, many believed in Him.

*Chapter 11*

¹There was a certain man who was very ill. He was known as Lazarus from Bethany, which is the hometown of Mary and her sister Martha. ²Mary *did a beautiful thing for Jesus. She* anointed the Lord with a pleasant-smelling oil and wiped His feet with her hair. Her brother Lazarus became deathly ill, ³so the sisters immediately sent a message to Jesus which said, "Lord, the one You love is very ill." ⁴Jesus heard the message:

**Jesus:** His sickness will not end in his death but will bring great glory to God. As these events unfold, the Son of God will be exalted.

⁵Jesus *dearly* loved Mary, Martha, and Lazarus. ⁶However, after receiving this news, He waited two more days where He was.

---

* 10:40 Literally, immerse, to show repentance

**Jesus** (*speaking to the disciples*): [7]It is time to return to Judea.

**Disciples:** [8]Teacher, the last time You were there, some Jews attempted to execute You by crushing You with stones. Why would You go back?

**Jesus:** [9]There are 12 hours of daylight, correct? If anyone walks in the day, that person does not stumble because he or she sees the light of the world. [10]If anyone walks at night, he will trip and fall, because he does not have the light within. [11](Jesus briefly pauses.) Our friend Lazarus has gone to sleep, so I will go to awaken him.

**Disciples:** [12]Lord, if he is sleeping, then he will be all right.

[13]Jesus used "sleep" *as a metaphor* for death, but the disciples took Him literally *and did not understand.* [14]Then, Jesus spoke plainly.

**Jesus:** Lazarus is dead, [15]and I am grateful for your sakes that I was not there when he died. Now you will *see and* believe. *It does not matter if the people there want to kill Me.* Gather yourselves, and let's go to him.

**Thomas, Didymus the Twin** (*to the disciples*): [16]Let's go so we can die with Him.

[17-18]As Jesus was approaching Bethany (which is about two miles east of Jerusalem), He heard that Lazarus had been in the tomb four days. [19]Now, many people had come to comfort Mary and Martha as they mourned the loss of their brother. [20]Martha went to meet Jesus when word arrived that He was approaching Bethany, but Mary stayed behind at the house.

**Martha:** [21]Lord, if You had been with us, my brother would not have died. [22]Even so, I still believe that anything You ask of God will be done.

**Jesus:** [23]Your brother will rise to life.

**Martha:** [24]I know. He will rise again when everyone is resurrected on the last day.

**Jesus:** [25]I am the resurrection and the source of all life; those who believe in Me will live even in death. [26]Everyone who lives and believes in Me will never truly die. Do you believe this?

**Martha:** [27]Yes, Lord, I believe that You are the Liberating King, God's own Son who *we have heard* is coming into the world.

[28]After this, Martha ran home to Mary.

**Martha** (*whispering to Mary*): Come with me. The Teacher is here, and He has asked for you.

[29]Mary did not waste a minute. She got up and went [30]to the same spot where Martha had found Jesus outside the village. [31]The people gathered in her home offering support and comfort assumed she was going back to the tomb to cry and mourn, so they followed her. [32]Mary approached Jesus, saw Him, and fell at His feet.

**Mary:** Lord, if only You had been here, my brother would still be alive.

[33]When Jesus saw Mary's *profound grief and the moaning and weeping of her companions*, He was deeply moved *by their pain* in His spirit and was intensely troubled.

**Jesus:** [34]Where have you laid his body?
**Jews:** Come and see, Lord.

[35]*As they walked,* Jesus wept; [36]and everyone noticed how much Jesus must have loved Lazarus. [37]But others were skeptical.

**Others:** If this man can give sight to the blind, He could have kept him from dying. *Why wasn't He here sooner if He loved Lazarus so much?*

[38]Then Jesus, who was intensely troubled by all of this, approached the tomb—a *small* cave covered by a *massive* stone.

**Jesus:** [39]Remove the stone.
**Martha:** Lord, he has been dead four days; the stench will be unbearable.

**Jesus:** [40]Remember, I told you that if you believe, you will see the glory of God.

[41]They removed the stone, and Jesus lifted His eyes toward heaven.

**Jesus:** Father, I am grateful that You have heard Me. [42]I know that You are always listening, but I proclaim it loudly so that everyone here will believe You have sent Me.

[43]After these words, He called out in a thunderous voice.

**Jesus:** Lazarus, come out!

[44]Then, the man who was dead walked out of his tomb bound from head to toe in a burial shroud.

**Jesus:** Untie him, and let him go.

*O*nce again, Jesus amazed us. How could He raise Lazarus? What kind of man was this who could speak life into death's darkness? Throughout His time with us, we were continually surprised by Jesus. He was obviously unique. He was unlike anyone we had met before. I remember the time Jesus was awakened from a peaceful rest and rose to face a fierce gale of wind and the stinging spray that came off the Sea of Galilee. Even the seasoned sailors among us were panicking. Jesus rebuked the storm and said, "That's enough! Be still!" Immediately the wind subsided. The rough sea became calm. Jesus turned to us and rebuked us for our lack of faith. In the wake of that storm, we talked among ourselves, asking, "Who is this Jesus? How can it be that He has power over even the wind and the waves? And how could He have power over death?"[3] It took us a while, but more and more we became convinced this was no ordinary man.

---

[3] Mark 4:35-41

⁴⁵As a result, many of the Jews who had come with Mary saw what happened and believed in Him. ⁴⁶But some went to the Pharisees to report what they witnessed Jesus doing. ⁴⁷As a result of these reports—*and on short notice*—the chief priests and Pharisees called a meeting of the high council.

**Pharisees:** What are we going to do about this man? He is performing many miracles. ⁴⁸If we don't stop this now, every man, woman, and child will believe in Him. *You know what will happen next? The Romans will think He's mounting a revolution and* will destroy our temple. It will be the end of our nation.

**Caiaphas, the High Priest that year:** ⁴⁹You have no idea what you are talking about; ⁵⁰what you don't understand is that it's better for you that one man should die for the people so the whole nation won't perish.

⁵¹*His speech was more than it seemed.* As high priest that year, Caiaphas prophesied (without knowing it) that Jesus would die on behalf of the entire nation, ⁵²and not just for the *children of Israel*—He would die so all God's children could be gathered from the four corners of the world into one people. ⁵³In that moment, they cemented their intentions to have Jesus executed.

⁵⁴From that day forward, Jesus refrained from walking publicly among the people in Judea. He withdrew to a small town known as Ephraim, a rural area near the wilderness, where He set up camp with His disciples.

⁵⁵The Passover was approaching, and Jews everywhere traveled to Jerusalem early so they could purify themselves and prepare for Passover. ⁵⁶People were looking for Jesus, hoping to catch a glimpse of Him in the city. All the while some Jews were discussing Him in the temple.

**Some Jews:** Do you think He will decide not to come *to Jerusalem this year* for the feast?

⁵⁷*In the midst of this confusion,* the Pharisees and the chief priests ordered that if anyone knew the whereabouts of Jesus

*of Nazareth*, it must be reported immediately so they could arrest Him.

*Chapter 12*

¹Six days before the Passover feast, Jesus journeyed to the village of Bethany, to the home of Lazarus, who had recently been raised from the dead, ²where they hosted Him for dinner. Martha was busy serving *as the hostess*, Lazarus reclined at the table with Him, ³and Mary took a pound of fine ointment, pure nard (which is *both rare and* expensive), and anointed Jesus' feet with it, and then wiped them with her hair. As the pleasant fragrance of this extravagant ointment filled the entire house, ⁴Judas Iscariot, one of His disciples (who was plotting to betray Jesus), began to speak.

**Judas Iscariot:** ⁵*How could she pour out* this vast amount of fine oil? Why didn't she sell it? It is worth nearly a year's wages;* the money could have been given to the poor.

⁶This had nothing to do with Judas's desire to help the poor. The truth is he served as the treasurer, and he helped himself to the money from the common pot at every opportunity.

**Jesus:** ⁷Leave her alone. She has observed this custom in anticipation of the day of My burial. ⁸The poor are ever present, but I will be leaving.

⁹Word spread of Jesus' presence, and a large crowd was gathering to see Jesus and the formerly deceased Lazarus, whom He had brought back from the dead. ¹⁰The chief priests were secretly plotting Lazarus's murder since, ¹¹because of him,

---

* 12:5 Greek *300 denarii*

many Jews were leaving their teachings and believing in Jesus.

[12]The next day, a great crowd of people who had come to the festival heard that Jesus was coming to Jerusalem, [13]so they gathered branches of palm trees to wave as they celebrated His arrival.

**Crowds** (*shouting*):

Hosanna!
He who comes in the name of the Lord is truly blessed*
    and is King of all Israel.

[14]Jesus found a young donkey, sat on it, *and rode through the crowds mounted on this small beast.* The Scriptures foretold of this day:

[15]Daughter of Zion, do not be afraid.
    Watch! Your King is coming.
    *You will find Him* seated on the colt of a donkey.*

[16]The disciples did not understand any of this at the time; these truths did not sink in until Jesus had been glorified. As they reflected on their memories of Jesus, they realized these things happened just as they were written. [17]Those who witnessed the resurrection of Lazarus enthusiastically spoke of Jesus to all who would listen, [18]and that is why the crowd went out to meet Him. They had heard of the miraculous sign He had done.

*W*e suspected during our time with Jesus that He was more than a man, but it took the power and glory of the resurrection to convince us completely that Jesus was divine. When we saw Him, when we touched Him, when the sound of His voice thundered in our souls, we knew we were face-to-face with God's immense glory, the unique Son of God. As we read and reread the

---

* 12:13 Psalm 118:26
* 12:15 Zechariah 9:9

> Scriptures in light of our experience of Him, we found that Jesus' life and story were the climax of God's covenants with His people.

**Pharisees** *(to one another)*: ¹⁹Our efforts to squelch Him have not worked, *but now is not the time for action.* Look, the world is following after Him.

²⁰Among the crowds traveling to Jerusalem were Greeks seeking to *follow God and* worship at the great feast. ²¹⁻²²Some of them came to Philip with an important request.

**Greek Pilgrims** *(to Philip)*: Sir, we are hoping to meet Jesus.

Philip, a disciple from the Galilean village of Bethsaida, told Andrew *that these Greeks were wanting to see Jesus.* Together Andrew and Philip approached Jesus to inform Him about the request.

**Jesus** *(to Philip and Andrew)*: ²³The time has come for the Son of Man to be glorified. ²⁴I tell you the truth: unless a grain of wheat is planted in the ground and dies, it remains a solitary seed. But when it is planted, it produces in death a great harvest. ²⁵The one who loves this life will lose it, and the one who despises it in this world will have life forevermore. ²⁶Anyone who serves Me must follow My path; anyone who serves Me will want to be where I am, and he will be honored by the Father. ²⁷My spirit is low and unsettled. How can I ask the Father to save Me from this hour? This hour is the purpose for which I have come *into the world. But what I can say is this:* ²⁸"Father, glorify Your name!"

Suddenly, a voice echoed from the heavens.

**The Father:** I have glorified My name. And again I will bring glory *in this hour that will resound throughout time.*

[29]The crowd of people surrounding Jesus were confused.

**Some in the Crowd:** It sounded like thunder.
**Others:** A heavenly messenger spoke to Him.
**Jesus:** [30]The Voice you hear has not spoken for My benefit, but for yours. [31]Now judgment comes upon this world, *and everything will change.* The tyrant of this world, *Satan,* will be thrown out. [32]When I am lifted up from the earth, then all of humanity will be drawn to Me.

[33]These words foreshadowed the nature of His death.

**Crowd:** [34]The law teaches that the Liberating King is the One who will remain without end. How can You say it is essential that the Son of Man be lifted up? Who is this Son of Man *You are talking about?*
**Jesus:** [35]Light is among you, but very soon it will flicker out. Walk as you have the light; and then the darkness will not surround you. Those who walk in darkness don't know where they are going. [36]While the light is with you, believe in the light and you will be reborn as sons *and daughters* of the light.

After speaking these words, Jesus left the people to go to a place of seclusion. [37]Despite all the signs He performed, they still did not believe in Him. [38]Isaiah spoke of this reality, saying,

> Lord, who could accept what we've been told?
> > And who has seen the awesome power of the Lord
> > revealed?[*]

[39]This is the reason they are unable to believe. [40]Isaiah also said,

> God has blinded their eyes,
> > and hardened their hearts
> So that their eyes cannot see *properly*
> > and their hearts cannot understand,
> > *and be persuaded*

---

* 12:38 Isaiah 53:1

> by *the truth* to turn to Me
> and be reconciled by My healing hand.<sup>*</sup>

<sup>41</sup>Isaiah could say this because he had seen the glory of the Lord *with his own eyes* and declared His beauty aloud. <sup>42</sup>Yet many leaders secretly believed in Him, but would not declare their faith because the Pharisees continued their threats to expel all His followers from the synagogue; <sup>43</sup>here's why: they loved to please men more than they desired to glorify God.

**Jesus** (*crying out before the people*): <sup>44</sup>Anyone who believes in Me is not placing his faith in Me, but in the One who sent Me here. <sup>45</sup>If one sees Me, he sees the One who sent Me. <sup>46</sup>I am here to bring light in this world, freeing everyone who believes in Me from the darkness *that blinds him.* <sup>47</sup>If anyone listening to My teachings chooses to ignore them, so be it: I have come to liberate the world, not to judge it. <sup>48</sup>However, those who reject Me and My teachings will be judged: in the last day, My words will be their judge. <sup>49</sup>Because I am not speaking *of My own volition and* from My own authority; the Father who sent Me has commanded Me what to say and speak. <sup>50</sup>I know His command is eternal life, so every word I utter originates in Him.

*Chapter 13*

<sup>1</sup>Before the Passover festival began, Jesus was keenly aware that His hour had come to depart from this world and to return to the Father. From beginning to end, Jesus' days were marked by His love for His people. <sup>2</sup>Before Jesus and His disciples gathered for dinner, the adversary filled Judas Iscariot's heart with plans of deceit and betrayal. <sup>3</sup>Jesus, knowing that He had come from God and was going away to

---

<sup>*</sup> 12:40 Isaiah 6:10

God, ⁴stood up from dinner and removed His outer garments. He then wrapped Himself in a towel, ⁵poured water in a basin, and began to wash the feet of the disciples, drying them with His towel.

**Simon Peter** (*as Jesus approaches*): ⁶Lord, are You going to wash my feet?

**Jesus:** ⁷Peter, you don't realize what I am doing, but you will understand later.

**Peter:** ⁸You will not wash my feet, now or ever!

**Jesus:** If I don't wash you, you will have nothing to do with Me.

**Peter:** ⁹Then wash me but don't stop with my feet. Cleanse my hands and head as well.

**Jesus:** ¹⁰Listen, anyone who has bathed is clean all over except for the feet. But I tell you this, not all of you are clean.

---

*M*y life changed that day; there was a new clarity about how I was supposed to live. I saw the world in a totally new way. The dirt, grime, sin, pain, rebellion, and torment around me were no longer impediments to the spiritual path.

Where I saw pain and filth, I found an opportunity to extend God's kingdom through an expression of love, humility, and service. This simple act of washing feet is a metaphor for the lens that Jesus gives us to see the world. He sees the people, the world He created—which He loves—He sees the filth, the corruption in the world that torments us. His mission is to cleanse those whom He loves from the horrors that torment them. This is His redemptive work with feet, families, disease, famine, and our hearts.

When Jesus saw disease, He saw the opportunity to heal. When He saw sin, He saw a chance to forgive and redeem. When He saw dirty feet, He saw a chance to wash them.

What do you see when you wander through the market,

---

along the streets, on the beaches, and through the slums?
Are you disgusted? Or do you seize the opportunity to
expand God's reign of love in the cosmos? This is what
Jesus did. The places we avoid, Jesus seeks.

[11]He knew the one with plans of betraying Him, which is why
He said, "not all of you are clean." [12]After washing their feet
and picking up His garments, He reclined at the table again.

**Jesus:** Do you understand what I have done to you? [13]You call
Me Teacher and Lord, and truly, that is who I am. [14]So if
your Lord and Teacher washes your feet, then you should
wash one another's feet. [15]I am your example; keep doing
what I do. [16]I tell you the truth: an emissary is not greater
than the master. Those who are sent are not greater than
the One who sends them. [17]If you know these things, and if
you put them into practice, you will find happiness. [18]I am
not speaking about all of you. I know whom I have chosen,
but let the Hebrew Scripture be fulfilled that says, "The
very same man who eats My bread with Me will stab Me in
the back."* [19]Assuredly, I tell you these truths before they
happen, so that when it all transpires you will believe that I
am. [20]I tell you the truth: anyone who accepts the ones I
send accepts Me. In turn, the ones who accept Me also
accept the One who sent Me.

[21]Jesus was becoming visibly distressed.

**Jesus:** I tell you the truth: one of you will betray Me.

[22]The disciples began to stare at one another, wondering who
was the unfaithful disciple. [23]One disciple in particular, who
was loved by Jesus, reclined next to Him at the table. [24]Peter
motioned to the disciple at Jesus' side.

**Peter** (*to the beloved disciple*): Find out who the betrayer is.

---

* 13:18 Psalm 41:9

**Beloved Disciple** (*leaning in to Jesus*): [25]Lord, who is it?

**Jesus:** [26]I will dip a piece of bread in My cup and give it to the one who will betray Me.

He dipped one piece in the cup and gave it to Judas, the son of Simon Iscariot. [27]After this occurred, Satan entered into Judas.

**Jesus** (*to Judas*): Make haste, and do what you are going to do.

[28]No one understood Jesus' instructions to Judas. [29]Because Judas carried the money, some thought he was being instructed to buy the necessary items for the feast, or give some money to the poor. [30]So Judas took his piece of bread and departed into the night.

[31]Upon Judas's departure, Jesus spoke:

**Jesus:** Now the Son of Man will be glorified as God is glorified in Him. [32]If God's glory is in Him, His glory is also in God. The moment of this astounding glory is imminent. [33]My children, My time here is brief. You will be searching for Me, and as I told the Jews, "You cannot go where I am going." [34]So I give you a new command: Love each other *deeply and fully*. Remember the ways that I have loved you, and demonstrate your love for others in those same ways. [35]Everyone will know you as My followers if you demonstrate your love to others.

**Simon Peter:** [36]Lord, where are You going?

**Jesus:** Peter, you cannot come with Me now, but later you will join Me.

**Peter:** [37]Why can't I go now? I'll give my life for You!

**Jesus:** [38]Will you really give your life for Me? I tell you the truth: you will deny Me three times before the rooster crows.

---

*U*ltimately, Peter was telling the truth. He was more than willing to lay down his life. But none of us understood the magnitude of the persecution and hatred that was about to be unleashed on all of us.

Even Peter, dear Peter, was afraid. He protested any

---

inference to Jesus' impending departure. We all would have done the same. Jesus calmed our fears over and over again with stories, metaphors, and outright promises, saying, "I would never abandon you like orphans. I will return to be with you."[4]

*Chapter 14*

**Jesus:** [1]Don't get lost in despair; believe in God and keep on believing in Me. [2]My Father's home is designed to accommodate all of you. If there were not room for everyone, I would have told you that. I am going to make arrangements for your arrival. [3]I will be there to personally greet you and welcome you home, where we will be together. [4]You know where I am going and how to get there.

**Thomas:** [5]Lord, we don't know where You are going, so how can we know the path?

**Jesus:** [6]I am the path, the truth, and the *energy of* life. No one comes to the Father except through Me. [7]If you know Me, you know the Father. Rest assured now; you know Him and have seen Him.

**Philip:** [8]Lord, all I am asking is that You show us the Father.

**Jesus** (to Philip): [9]I have lived with you all this time and you still don't know who I am? If you have seen Me, you have seen the Father. How can you keep asking to see the Father? [10]Don't you believe Me when I say I abide in the Father and the Father dwells in Me? I'm not making this up as I go along. The Father has given Me these truths that I have been speaking to you, and He empowers all My actions. [11]Accept these truths: I am in the Father and the Father is in Me. If you have trouble believing based on My words, believe because of the things I have done. [12]I tell you the

---

[4] John 14:18

truth: whoever believes in Me will be able to do what I have done, but they will do even greater things, because I will return to be with the Father. [13]Whatever you ask for in My name, I will do it so that the Father will get glory from the Son. [14]*Let Me say it again:* if you ask for anything in My name, I will do it. [15]If you love Me, obey the commandments I have given you. [16]I will ask the Father to send you another Helper, *the Spirit of truth,* who will remain constantly with you. [17]The world does not recognize the Spirit of truth, because it does not know the Spirit and is unable to receive Him. But you do know the Spirit because He lives with you, and He will dwell in you. [18]I will never abandon you like orphans; I will return to be with you. [19]In a little while, the world will not see Me, but I will not vanish completely from your sight. Because I live, you will also live. [20]At that time, you will know that I am in the Father, you are in Me, and I am in you. [21]The one who loves Me will do the things I have commanded. My Father loves everyone who loves Me, and I will love you and reveal My heart, will, and nature to you.

---

*G*od became flesh and lived among us, not just to have a transaction with us and ultimately die, but to continue to be with us even when He didn't have to and to send His Spirit to be present with us. So, in that, God calls us to something greater, something more significant: We are here as redeeming forces on this earth; our time here is about reclaiming the things He has created. We believe that God has created the entire cosmos; our work here is to say, "This belongs to God," and to help point out the beauty of creation to everyone we know, everyone we meet. And most of all, to live in it ourselves.

---

**The Other Judas:** [22]Lord, why will You reveal Yourself to us, but not to the world?

**Jesus:** [23]Anyone who loves Me will listen to My voice and obey. The Father will love him, and We will draw close to him and make a dwelling place within him. [24]The one who does not love Me ignores My message, which is not from Me, but from the Father who sent Me.

²⁵I have spoken these words while I am here with you. ²⁶The Father is sending a great Helper, the Holy Spirit, in My name to teach you everything and to remind you of all I have said to you. ²⁷My peace is the legacy I leave to you. I don't give gifts like those of this world. Do not let your heart be troubled or fearful. ²⁸You were listening when I said, "I will go away, but I will also return to be with you." If you love Me, celebrate the fact that I am going to be with the Father because He is far greater than I am. ²⁹I have told you all these things in advance so that your faith will grow as these things come to pass. ³⁰I am almost finished speaking to you. The one who rules the world is stepping forward and he has no part in Me, ³¹but to demonstrate to the cosmos My love for the Father, I will do just as He commands. Stand up. It is time for us to leave this place.

---

*T*he Holy Spirit planted the teachings of our Lord into our very beings. God would now dwell in the hearts of all true believers, and the chasm between God and humanity would be bridged. As you can imagine, the idea of Jesus leaving us created a whirlwind of fear and doubt. But once again, Jesus reached in gently and calmed our storms when He said, "I will now dwell inside of you." A connection is made between God and us, much like the first days in the garden—God the Creator strolling in paradise with Adam. God is, once again in Jesus and the Holy Spirit, present amid suffering, hope, sin, and friendship.

---

*Chapter 15*

**Jesus:** ¹I am the true vine, and My Father is the keeper of the vineyard. ²My Father examines every branch in Me and cuts away those who do not bear fruit. He leaves those bearing fruit and carefully prunes them so that they will bear more fruit; ³already, you are clean because you have heard My voice. ⁴Abide in Me, and I will abide in you. A branch cannot bear fruit if it is disconnected from the vine, and neither will you if you are not connected to Me.

⁵I am the vine, and you are the branches. If you abide in Me and I in you, you will bear great fruit. Without Me, you will accomplish nothing. ⁶If anyone does not abide in Me, he is like a branch that is tossed out and shrivels up, and is later gathered to be tossed into the fire to burn. ⁷If you abide in Me and My voice abides in you, anything you ask will come to pass for you. ⁸Your abundant growth and your faithfulness as My followers will bring glory to the Father.

*A*t a time when all of us were feeling as if we were about to be uprooted, Jesus sketched out a picture for us of this new life as a flourishing vineyard—a labyrinth of vines and strong branches steeped in rich soil, abundant grapes hanging from their vines ripening in the sun. Jesus sculpted out a new garden of Eden in our imaginations—one that was bustling with fruit, sustenance, and satisfying aromas. This is the Kingdom life. It is all about connection, sustenance, and beauty.

**Jesus:** ⁹I have loved you as the Father has loved Me. Abide in My love. ¹⁰Follow My example in obeying the Father's commandments and receiving His love. If you obey My commandments, you will stay in My love. ¹¹I want you to know the delight I experience, to find ultimate satisfaction, which is why I am telling you all of this.

¹²My commandment to you is this: love others as I have loved you. ¹³There is no greater way to love than to give your life for your friends. ¹⁴You celebrate our friendship if you obey this command. ¹⁵I don't call you servants any longer; servants don't know what the master is doing, but I have told you everything the Father has said to Me. I call

you friends. ¹⁶You did not choose Me. I chose you, and I orchestrated all of this so that you would be sent out and bear great and perpetual fruit. As you do this, anything you ask the Father in My name will be done. ¹⁷This is My command to you: love one another.

¹⁸If you find that the world despises you, remember that before it despised you, it first despised Me. ¹⁹If you were a product of the world order, then it would love you. But you are not a product of the world because I have taken you out of it, and it despises you for that very reason. ²⁰Don't forget what I have spoken to you: "a servant is not superior to the master." If I was mistreated, you should expect nothing less. If they accepted what I have spoken, they will also hear you. ²¹Everything they do to you they will do on My account because they do not know the One who has sent Me. ²²If I had not spoken within their hearing, they would not be guilty of sin, but now they have no excuse for ignoring My voice.

²³If someone despises Me, he also despises My Father. ²⁴If I had not demonstrated things for them that have never been done, they would not be guilty of sin. But the reality is they have stared Me in the face, and they have despised Me and the Father nonetheless. ²⁵Yet, their law, which says, "They despised Me without any cause,"* has again been proven true.

²⁶I will send a great Helper to you from the Father, one known as the Spirit of truth. He comes from the Father and will point to the truth as it concerns Me. ²⁷But you will also point others to the truth about My identity, because you have journeyed with Me since this all began.

---

*A*s Jesus warns us of the mistreatment we can expect, He disarms our fears by reminding us of the most important things. If the Spirit is in us, we have no reason to fear. In fact, the church will thrive under persecution. Yet we are obsessed with power and political

---

* 15:25 Psalm 35:19

prominence as a means to influence the culture. As Christian citizens, we have an obligation to actively strive for justice and freedom. But how will that happen?

Listen carefully, for this is the wisdom God has given to each generation. Lasting justice and morality cannot be lobbied for or legislated. It is a result of the Holy Spirit's work in the lives of those of us who learn that God loves us. So take heed, lest we forget these important labors are always secondary to the gospel and at times even affect the cause of the Liberating King negatively. True Christianity, the real work of the Kingdom, often thrives under fierce attack and opposition. Jesus announced this coming persecution to us, His followers, believing this will lead to our finest hour.

*Chapter 16*

**Jesus:** [1]I am telling you all of this so that you may avoid the offenses that are coming. [2]The time will come when they will kick you out of the synagogue because some believe God desires them to execute you as an act of faithful service. [3]They will do this because they don't know the Father, or else they would know Me. [4]I'm telling you all this so that when it comes to pass you will remember what you have heard. It was not important for Me to give you this information in the beginning when I was with you. [5]But now, I am going to the One who has sent Me, and none of you ask Me, "Where are You going?"

[6]I know that hearing news like this is overwhelming and sad. [7]But the truth is that My departure will be a gift that will serve you well, because if I don't leave, the great Helper will not come to your aid. When I leave, I will send Him to you. [8-9]When He arrives, He will uncover the sins of the

world, expose unbelief as sin, and allow all to see their sins in the light of righteousness for the first time. ¹⁰This new awareness of righteousness is important because I am going to the Father and will no longer be present with you. ¹¹The Spirit will also carry My judgment because the one who rules in this world has already been defeated.

¹²I have so much more to say, but you cannot absorb it right now. ¹³⁻¹⁵The Spirit of truth will come and guide you in all truth. He will not speak His own words to you; He will speak what He hears, revealing to you the things to come and bringing glory to Me. The Spirit has unlimited access to Me, to all that I possess and know, just as everything the Father has is Mine. That is the reason I am confident He will care for My own and reveal the path to you. ¹⁶For a little while you will not see Me, but after that, a time will come when you will see Me again.

**Some of His Disciples:** ¹⁷What does He mean? "I'll be here, and then I won't be here, because I'll be with the Father."

**Other Disciples:** ¹⁸What is He saying? "A little while"? We don't understand.

---

*T*he promise of eternity is a reminder that we were made for another world. We found great comfort amid our fear, knowing we would be reunited with our Liberating King and joined with the Father. As we labor together in this world—enduring pain, loss, and unfulfilled desires—be encouraged that in eternity all our needs will be fulfilled in the presence of God.

---

¹⁹Jesus knew they had questions to ask of Him, so He approached them.

**Jesus:** Are you trying to figure out what I mean when I say you will see Me in a little while? ²⁰I tell you the truth, a time is approaching when you will weep and mourn while the world is celebrating. You will grieve, but that grief will give birth to great joy. ²¹⁻²²In the same way that a woman labors in great pain during childbirth, only to forget the intensity of the pain when she holds her child, when I return, your labored grief will also change into a joy that cannot be stolen.

[23]When all this transpires, you will finally have the answers you have been seeking. I tell you the truth, anything you ask of the Father in My name, He will give to you. [24]Until this moment, you have not sought after anything in My name. Ask and you will receive, so that you will be filled with joy.

[25]I have been teaching you all of these truths through stories and metaphors, but the time is coming for Me to speak openly and directly of the Father.

[26]The day is coming when you will make a request in My name, but I will not represent you before the Father. [27]*You will be heard directly by the Father*. The Father loves you because you love Me and know that I come from the Father. [28]I came from the Father into the cosmos, but soon I will leave it and return to the Father.

*A*ll of us disciples mourned Jesus' refusal to take His rightful place as a king and lead a revolution. Jesus knew that political might, brute force, and earthly governments are not helpful tools in a battle for hearts. Spiritual revolutions are subversive. They are led by defiant acts of love (e.g., healing, foot washing, and martyrdom). Laws do not change hearts, and violence induces hatred and fear. But a sincere community of faith in which love and hope are demonstrated even in the darkest hours will lead a spiritual revolution. It is time we go forward with open eyes and continue to labor as Christian citizens, placing our hope only in the redemptive work of the gospel.

**Disciples:** [29]We hear You speaking clearly and not in metaphors. *How could we misunderstand?* [30]We see now that You are aware of everything and You reveal things at the proper time. So we do not need to question You, because we believe You have come from God.

**Jesus:** [31]So you believe now? [32]Be aware that a time is coming when you will be scattered *like seeds*. You will return to your own way, and I will be left alone. But I will not be alone, because the Father will be with Me. [33]I have told you these things so that you will be *whole and* at peace. In this world you will be plagued with times of trouble, but you need not fear; I have triumphed over this corrupt world order.

*G*enerations from now, believers will struggle to understand how they are connected to God and one another. They will see themselves as autonomous individuals, free agents who choose whatever allegiances suit them. Those of us who walked with Jesus had a different perspective. Maybe it came from our culture. Maybe it came from our faith. Probably both. We already saw ourselves as dependent on and connected to other people. We belonged to a family, a tribe, a people. To know who we were, we didn't look inside ourselves; we looked to others because they knew us and we were part of them. No one needed to "find himself" because he already knew. Our identities were tied up completely with others. The very nature of humans is that we grow from within another human, taking on the characteristics of our parents who connect us back to hundreds of generations. When Jesus entered our lives, none of this changed; yet all of it changed. He became the center of our lives. We now belonged to Him.

*Chapter 17*

**Jesus** (*lifting His face to the heavens*): [1]Father, My time has come. Glorify Your Son, and I will bring You great glory

²⁻³because You have given Me total authority over humanity. *I have come bearing the plentiful gifts of God,* and all that receive Me will experience everlasting life, a new intimate relationship with You, the one true God, and Jesus the Liberating King (the One You have sent). ⁴I have glorified You on earth and fulfilled the mission You set before Me.

⁵In this moment, Father, fuse Our collective glory and bring Us together as We were before creation existed. ⁶You have entrusted Me with these men who have come out of this corrupt world order. I have told them about Your nature and declared Your name to them, and they have held on to Your words and understood that these words, ⁷like everything else You have given Me, come from You. ⁸It is true, that these men You gave Me have received the words that come from You, and not only understood them but also believed that You sent Me. ⁹I am now making an appeal to You on their behalf. This request is not for the entire world; it is for those whom You have given to Me because they are Yours. ¹⁰Yours and Mine, Mine and Yours, for all that are Mine are Yours. Through them I have been glorified.

¹¹I will no longer be physically present in this world, but they will remain in this world. As I return to be with You, holy Father, remain with them through Your name, *the name You have given Me.* May they be one even as We are one. ¹²While I was physically present with them, I protected them through Your name, *which You have shared with Me.* I watched over them closely; and only one was lost, the one the Scriptures said was the son of destruction. ¹³Now I am returning to You. I am speaking this prayer here in the created cosmos *alongside friends and foes* so that in hearing it they might be consumed with joy. ¹⁴I have given them Your word; and the world has despised them because they are not products of the world, in the same way that I am not a product of the corrupt world order. ¹⁵Do not take them out of this world; protect them from the evil one.

¹⁶Like Me, they are not products of the corrupt world order. ¹⁷Immerse them in the truth, the truth Your voice speaks. ¹⁸In the same way You sent Me into this world, I am

sending them. <sup>19</sup>It is entirely for their benefit that I have set Myself apart, so that they may be set apart by truth. <sup>20</sup>I am not asking solely for their benefit; this prayer is also for all the believers who will follow them and hear them speak. <sup>21</sup>Father, may they all be one as You are in Me and I am in You; may they be in Us, for by this unity the world will believe that You sent Me.

<sup>22</sup>All the glory You have given to Me, I pass on to them. May that glory unify them and make them one as We are one, <sup>23</sup>I in them and You in Me, that they may be refined so that all will know that You sent Me, and You love them in the same way You love Me.

<sup>24</sup>Father, I long for the time when those You have given Me can join Me in My place so they may witness My glory, which comes from You. You have loved Me before the foundations of the cosmos were laid. <sup>25</sup>Father, You are just; though this corrupt world order does not know You, I do. These followers know that You have sent Me. <sup>26</sup>I have told them about Your nature; and I will continue to speak of Your name, in order that Your love, which was poured out on Me, will be in them. And I will also be in them.

## Chapter 18

<sup>1</sup>When Jesus finished praying, He began a brief journey with His disciples to the other side of the Kidron Valley, a deep ravine that floods in the winter rains, then farther on to a garden where He gathered His disciples.

<sup>2-3</sup>Judas Iscariot (who had already set his betrayal in motion and knew that Jesus often met with the disciples in this olive grove) entered the garden with an entourage of Roman soldiers and officials sent by the chief priests and Pharisees. They brandished their weapons under the light of

torches and lamps. [4]Jesus stepped forward. It was clear He was not surprised because He knew all things.

**Jesus:** Whom are you looking for?
**Judas's Entourage:** [5]Jesus the Nazarene.
**Jesus:** I am the One.

Judas, the betrayer, stood with the military force. [6]As Jesus spoke "I am the One," the forces fell back on the ground. [7]Jesus asked them a second time:

**Jesus:** Whom are you searching for?
**Judas's Entourage:** Jesus the Nazarene.
**Jesus:** [8]I have already said that I am the One. If it is I you are looking for, then let these men go free.

[9]This happened to fulfill the promise He made that none of those entrusted to Him will be lost.* [10]Suddenly Peter lunged toward Malchus, one of the high priest's servants, and, with his sword, severed the man's right ear.

**Jesus** (*to Peter*): [11]Put down your sword and return it to the sheath. Am I to turn away from the cup the Father has given Me to drink?

[12]So the Roman commander, soldiers, and Jewish officials arrested Jesus, cuffed His hands and feet, [13]and brought Him to Annas (the father-in-law of Caiaphas the high priest). [14]You may remember that Caiaphas counseled to the Jews that one should die for all people. [15-16]Simon Peter and another disciple followed behind Jesus. When they arrived, Peter waited in the doorway while the other disciple was granted access because of his relationship with the high priest. That disciple spoke to the woman at the door, and Peter was allowed inside.

**Servant Girl** (*to Peter*): [17]You are one of this man's disciples, aren't you?
**Peter:** I am not.

* 18:9 John 6:39

¹⁸All the servants and officers gathered around a charcoal fire to keep warm. It was a cold day, and Peter made his way into the circle to warm himself.

**Annas** (*to Jesus*): ¹⁹Who are Your disciples, and what do You teach?

**Jesus:** ²⁰I have spoken in public where the world can hear, always teaching in the synagogue and in the temple where the Jewish people gather. I have never spoken in secret. ²¹So why would you need to interrogate Me? Many have heard Me teach. Why don't you question them? They know what I have taught.

²²While Jesus offered His response, an officer standing nearby struck Jesus with his hand.

**Officer:** Is that how You speak to the high priest?

**Jesus:** ²³If I have spoken incorrectly, why don't you point out the untruths that I speak? Why do you hit Me if what I have said is correct?

²⁴Annas sent Jesus to Caiaphas bound as a prisoner. ²⁵As this was happening, Peter was still warming himself by the fire.

**Servants and Officers:** You too are one of His disciples, aren't you?

**Peter:** No, I am not.

²⁶One of the high priest's servants was related to the one assaulted by Peter.

**Servant of the High Priest, a relative of Malchus:** Didn't I see you in the garden with Him?

²⁷Peter denied it again, and instantly a rooster crowed.
   ²⁸Before the sun had risen, Jesus was taken from Caiaphas to the governor's palace. The Jewish leaders would not enter the palace because their presence in a Roman office would defile them and cause them to miss the Passover feast. Pilate, the governor, met them outside.

*N*ow Caiaphas was high priest at this time. The sacred office he occupied had been corrupted for more than a century by Jewish collaboration with Greeks and Romans. Reformers were few, and they had been unable to cleanse the high office from its pollutants. Because of this, many Jews had stopped coming to the temple. How could God's holy habitation on earth be pure if its primary representative was coddling the enemies of Israel? Caiaphas knew he needed friends in high places to put an end to Jesus. So he turned to Pilate, the Roman governor. It was his job to look out for Roman interests in Judea. History records that he was an irritable man, unnecessarily cruel and intentionally provocative. Many Jews died on his watch. For Pilate, Jesus would be just one more.

**Pilate:** [29]What charges do you bring against this man?
**Priests and Officials:** [30]If He weren't a lawbreaker, we wouldn't have brought Him to you.
**Pilate:** [31]Then judge Him yourselves, by your own law.
**Jews:** Our authority does not allow us to give Him the death penalty.

[32]All these things were a fulfillment of the words Jesus had spoken indicating the way that He would die. [33]So Pilate re-entered the governor's palace and called for Jesus to follow him.

*I*nitially, Pilate told the Jewish leaders to take Jesus and try Him according to our own laws, but when they hinted at capital charges, Pilate agreed to interrogate Jesus. Rome reserved the right to decide who lived and died in the provinces. They didn't delegate that to the Jewish high council. The charge of blasphemy carried no weight in Roman jurisprudence for it was a matter of our Jewish religious law. Rome had no opinion on such matters. So a new charge must be concocted, a charge that

> Rome did care about. Rome did care about taxes, of course, and took a dim view of anyone making royal claims under their noses.
>
> Pilate agreed to hear the charge, not wasting a Roman minute. He took Jesus inside and began asking Him about these charges.

**Pilate:** Are You the King of the Jews?

**Jesus:** [34]Are you asking Me because you believe this is true, or have others said this about Me?

**Pilate:** [35]I'm not a Jew, am I? Your people, including the chief priests, have arrested You and placed You in my custody. What have You done?

**Jesus:** [36]My kingdom is not recognized in this world. If this were My kingdom, My servants would be fighting for My freedom. But My kingdom is not in this physical realm.

**Pilate:** [37]So You are a king?

**Jesus:** You say that I am king. For this I have been born, and for this I have come into the cosmos, to demonstrate the power of truth. Everyone who seeks truth hears My voice.

**Pilate** (*to Jesus*): [38]What is truth?

Pilate left Jesus to go and speak to the Jewish people.

**Pilate** (*to the Jews*): I have not found any cause for charges to be brought against this man. [39]Your custom is that I should release a prisoner to you each year in honor of the Passover celebration; shall I release the King of the Jews to you?

**Jews:** [40]No, not this man! Give us Barabbas!

You should know that Barabbas was a terrorist.

> *I*'d like to have been a fly on the wall when Pilate had that private moment with Jesus. Pilate was interrogating Jesus like the man he was: an insecure and cruel power broker representing Roman interests in our land. Jesus,

though, was doing His typical mustard seed bit, speaking right over the head of the man who later would show Him no mercy. Pilate couldn't handle the truth when he asked, "Are You the King of the Jews?" Jesus was the King of the Jews. And that was the truth. Although Pilate wouldn't recognize it, He was his King too. But as Jesus knew, the world didn't recognize His kingdom. That's because it was sourced in heaven above, not in Rome. His authority came from God the Father, Creator, Sustainer—not from the Roman senate.

*Chapter 19*

¹Pilate took Jesus and had Him flogged. ²The soldiers twisted thorny branches together as a crown and placed it onto His brow and wrapped Him in a purple cloth. ³They drew near to Him, shouting:

**Soldiers** (*striking at Jesus*): Bow down, everyone! This is the King of the Jews!
**Pilate** (*going out to the crowd*): ⁴Listen, I stand in front of you with this man to make myself clear: I find this man innocent of any crimes.

⁵Then Jesus was paraded out before the people, wearing the crown of thorns and the purple robe.

**Pilate:** Here is the man!
**Chief Priests and Officers** (*shouting*): ⁶Crucify, crucify!
**Pilate:** You take Him and crucify Him; I have declared Him not guilty of any punishable crime!
**Jews:** ⁷Our law says that He should die because He claims to be the Son of God.

[8]Pilate was terrified to hear the Jews making their claims for His execution, [9]so he retired to his court, the Praetorium.

**Pilate** *(to Jesus)*: Where are You from?

Jesus did not speak.

**Pilate:** [10]How can You ignore me? Are You not aware that I have the authority to either free You or crucify You?
**Jesus:** [11]Any authority you have over Me comes from above, not from your political position. Because of this the one who handed Me to you is guilty of the greater sin.

[12]Pilate listened to Jesus' words; and, taking them to heart, he attempted to release Jesus, but the Jews opposed him, shouting:

**Jews:** If you release this man, you have betrayed Caesar. Anyone who claims to be a king threatens Caesar's throne.

[13]After Pilate heard these accusations, he sent Jesus out and took his seat in the place where he rendered judgment. This place was called the Pavement, or Gabbatha in Hebrew. [14]All this occurred at the sixth hour on the day everyone prepares for the Passover.

**Pilate** *(to the Jews)*: Look, here is your King!
**Jews:** [15]Put Him away; crucify Him!
**Pilate:** You want me to crucify your King?
**Chief Priests:** We have no king but Caesar!

[16]Pilate handed Him over to his soldiers knowing that He would be crucified. [17]They sent Jesus out carrying His own instrument of execution, the cross, to a hill known as the place of the skull, or Golgotha in Hebrew. [18]In that place they crucified Him along with two others. One was on His right and the other on His left. [19]Pilate ordered that a plaque be placed above Jesus' head. It read, "Jesus of Nazareth, King of the Jews." [20]Because the site was near an urban region, it was

THE VOICE REVEALED

written in three languages (Greek, Latin, and Hebrew) so that all could understand.

**Chief Priests** *(to Pilate)*: [21]Don't write, "The King of the Jews." Write, "He said, 'I am King of the Jews'!"
**Pilate:** [22]I have written what I have written.

[23]As Jesus was being crucified, the soldiers tore His outer garments into four pieces, one for each of them. They wanted to do the same with His tunic; but it was seamless, one piece of fabric woven from the top down. [24]So they said,

**Soldier** *(to other soldiers)*: Don't tear it. Let's cast lots, and the winner will take the whole thing.

This happened in keeping with the Hebrew Scriptures, which said, "They divided My outer garments and cast lots for My clothes."[*] These soldiers did exactly what was foretold in the Hebrew Scriptures. [25]Jesus' mother was standing next to His cross along with her sister, Mary the wife of Clopas, and Mary Magdalene. [26]Jesus looked to see His mother, and the disciple He loved, standing nearby.

**Jesus** *(to Mary, His mother)*: Dear woman, this is your son *(motioning to the beloved disciple)*! [27]This is now your mother *(to His disciple)*!

---

*N*ow you know who "the beloved disciple" is, the last eyewitness to the life, death, and resurrection of Jesus. Mary became family to me, fulfilling the dying wish of Jesus, my Savior. For those of us who gathered at the foot of the cross, family was less about blood kinship than it was about covenant obedience.

Caring for her was never a burden, and the reality is that she has always been a simple and private woman. God made her the vessel to bring His Son into the world,

---

[*] 19:24 Psalm 22:18

and her love for Him was warm and beautiful. Part of me is protective of her, as a son naturally is of his mother. Still, I can see why those who didn't know her would want to learn more about this remarkable woman, especially those grieving over their own losses. Surely they are looking for answers to how to move forward in their own lives. The mother of our Lord served the redemptive purposes of her son and the Savior of us all until her last day on earth.

When I would feel sorry for myself, I just had to think about Jesus. He spent all this time before His death, and through His death, showing us how to love and how to serve. He was asking me to do no more in serving Mary than He did in serving us.

From that moment the disciple treated her like his own mother and welcomed her into his house. [28]Jesus knew now that His work had been accomplished, and the Hebrew Scriptures were being fulfilled.

**Jesus:** I am thirsty.

[29]A jar of sour wine had been left there, so they took a hyssop branch with a sponge soaked in the vinegar and put it to His mouth. [30]When Jesus drank, He spoke:

**Jesus:** It is finished!

In that moment, His head fell, and He gave up the spirit. [31]The Jews asked Pilate to have their legs broken so the bodies would not remain on the crosses on the Sabbath. It was the day of preparation for the Passover, and that year the Passover fell on the Sabbath. [32]The soldiers came and broke the legs of both the men crucified next to Jesus. [33]When they came up to Jesus' cross, they could see that He was dead, so they did not break His legs. [34]Instead, one soldier took his spear and pierced His abdomen, which brought a gush of blood and water.

<sup>35</sup>This testimony is true; in fact, it is an eyewitness account, and he has reported what he saw so that you also may believe. <sup>36</sup>It happened this way to fulfill the Hebrew Scriptures that "not one of His bones shall be broken"*; <sup>37</sup>and the Hebrew Scriptures also say, "they will look upon Him whom they pierced."*

<sup>38</sup>After all this, Joseph of Arimathea, a disciple who kept his faith a secret for fear of the Jewish officials, made a request to Pilate for the body of Jesus. Pilate granted his request, and Joseph retrieved the body. <sup>39</sup>Nicodemus, who first came to Jesus under the cloak of darkness, brought over 100 pounds of myrrh and ointments for His burial. <sup>40</sup>Together, they took Jesus' body and wrapped Him in linens soaked in essential oils and spices, according to Jewish burial customs.

<sup>41</sup>Near the place He was crucified, there was a garden with a newly prepared tomb. <sup>42</sup>Because it was the day of preparation, they arranged to lay Jesus in this tomb so they could rest on the Sabbath.

---

As the lifeless body of Jesus was laid into the virgin tomb, those of us who witnessed the spectacle retreated into the city that had claimed the lives of so many prophets. All of us were crushed that our teacher and friend had died such a horrible death. Our hopes were dashed against the rocks of Golgotha. In the first hours of our grief, we huddled together in secret in the city, hoping to avoid our own arrests and executions. We mourned. We grieved. We remembered. Three days later, some of us ventured outside the city and returned to the place where He was buried. Miraculously, the stone was rolled back and the rock-hewn tomb was empty. Had someone taken His body? Were His enemies laying a trap for us? Or perhaps—could it be—that the last days were here?

Now I want you to know what I remember of that glorious day.

---

* 19:36 Exodus 12:46; Numbers 9:12; Psalm 34:20
* 19:37 Zechariah 12:10

¹Before the sun had risen on Sunday morning, Mary Magdalene made a trip to the tomb where His body was laid to rest. In the darkness, she discovered the covering had been rolled away. ²She darted out of the garden to find Simon Peter and the dearly loved disciple to deliver this startling news.

**Mary Magdalene:** They have taken the body of our Lord, and we cannot find Him!

³Together they all departed for the tomb to see for themselves. ⁴They began to run, and Peter could not keep up. The beloved disciple arrived first ⁵but did not go in. There was no corpse in the tomb, only the linens and cloths He was wrapped in. ⁶When Simon Peter finally arrived, he went into the tomb and observed the same: ⁷the cloth that covered His face appeared to have been folded carefully and placed, not with the linen cloths, but to the side. ⁸After Peter pointed this out, the other disciple (who had arrived long before Peter) also entered the tomb and, based on what he saw, faith began to well up inside him! ⁹Before this moment, none of them understood the Scriptures and why He must be raised from the dead. ¹⁰Then they all went to their homes.

¹¹Mary, however, stood outside the tomb, sobbing, crying, and kneeling at the entrance of the tomb. ¹²As she cried, two heavenly messengers appeared before her sitting where Jesus' head and feet had been laid.

**Heavenly Messengers:** ¹³Dear woman, why are you weeping?
**Mary Magdalene:** They have taken away my Lord, and I cannot find Him.

¹⁴After uttering these words, she turned around to see Jesus standing before her; but she did not recognize Him.

**Jesus:** [15]Dear woman, why are you sobbing? Who is it you are looking for?

She still had no idea who it was before her. Thinking He was the gardener, she muttered:

**Mary Magdalene:** Sir, if you are the one who carried Him away, then tell me where He is and I will retrieve Him.

**Jesus:** [16]Mary!

**Mary Magdalene** (*she turns to Jesus and tries to hug Him, speaking in Hebrew*): Rabboni, my Teacher!

**Jesus:** [17]Mary, you cannot hold Me. I must rise above this world to be with My Father, who is also your Father, My God, who is also your God. Go tell this to all My brothers.

[18]Mary Magdalene obeyed and went directly to His disciples.

---

*T*he hope of resurrection had often been a topic on the lips of Jesus. Now it was taking shape in our time. Confusion gave way to conviction as Jesus appeared to us alive over the next few Sundays. One by one He convinced us that God had raised Him from the dead.

---

**Mary Magdalene** (*announcing to the disciples*): I have seen the Lord, and this is what He said to me . . .

[19]On that same evening (Resurrection Sunday), the followers gathered together behind locked doors in fear that some of the Jewish leaders in Jerusalem were still searching for them. Out of nowhere, Jesus appeared in the center of the room.

**Jesus:** May each one of you be at peace.

[20]As He was speaking, He revealed the wounds in His hands and side. The disciples began to celebrate as it sunk in that they were really seeing the Lord.

**Jesus:** [21]I give you the gift of peace. In the same way the Father sent Me, I am now sending you.

²²Now He drew close enough to each of them that *they could feel His breath*. He breathed on them:

**Jesus:** Welcome the Holy Spirit of the living God. ²³You now have the mantle of God's forgiveness. As you go, you are able to share the life-giving power to forgive sins, or withhold forgiveness.

²⁴All of the eleven were present with the exception of Thomas. ²⁵He heard the accounts of each brother's interaction with the Lord.

**The Other Disciples:** We have seen the Lord!
**Thomas:** Until I see His hands, feel the wounds of the nails, and put my hand to His side, I won't believe what you are saying.

²⁶Eight days later, they gathered again behind locked doors and Jesus reappeared. This time Thomas was with them.

**Jesus:** May each one of you be at peace.

²⁷He drew close to Thomas and said:

**Jesus:** Reach out and touch Me. See the punctures in My hands; reach out your hand and put it to My side; leave behind your faithlessness and believe.
**Thomas** (*filled with emotion*): ²⁸You are the one true God and Lord of my life.
**Jesus:** ²⁹Thomas, you have faith because you have seen Me. Blessed are all those who never see Me and yet they still believe.

³⁰Jesus performed many other wondrous signs that are not written in this book. ³¹The accounts are recorded so that you, too, might believe that Jesus the Liberating King is the Son of God, because believing grants you the life He came to share.

## Chapter 21

After Jesus' death, we didn't know what to do with ourselves. What we all knew was fishing. So—we went fishing. Jesus never taught us how to turn two fish into a mound of food that could feed thousands, and we had no money. So, if we wanted to eat, then we had to go catch some fish. Grief has a way of stripping you down to basic survival skills. We were still trying to wrap our brains around what happened and why. We couldn't even catch our own bait!

We were a band of fishermen who were lost and lonely. But just when we thought things couldn't become stranger, Jesus showed up. He told us to fish on the other side of the boat. We did, and we were suddenly overwhelmed with fish. The nets were bulging.

What He showed us here, is that not only would our old ways of living leave us as empty as our nets, but our old habits were not going to work for us anymore. He had impacted our lives in a way that changed us forever. We couldn't go back. And He knew we didn't know how to go forward.

¹There was one other time when Jesus appeared to the disciples—this time by the Sea of Tiberias. This is how it happened: ²Simon Peter, Thomas (called Didymus), Nathanael (the Galilean from Cana), the sons of Zebedee, and two other disciples were together.

**Simon Peter** *(to disciples)*: ³I am going fishing.
**Disciples:** Then we will come with you.

They went out in the boat and caught nothing through the night. ⁴As day was breaking, Jesus was standing on the beach, but they did not know it was Jesus.

**Jesus:** <sup>5</sup>My sons, you haven't caught any fish, have you?
**Disciples:** No.
**Jesus:** <sup>6</sup>Throw your net on the starboard side of the boat, and your nets will find the fish.

They did what He said, and suddenly they could not lift their net because of the massive weight of the fish that filled it. <sup>7</sup>The disciple loved by Jesus turned to Peter and said:

**Beloved Disciple:** It is the Lord.

Immediately, when Simon Peter heard these words, he threw on his shirt (which he would take off while he was working) and dove into the sea. <sup>8</sup>The rest of the disciples followed him, bringing in the boat and dragging in their net full of fish. They were close to the shore, fishing only about 100 yards out. <sup>9</sup>When they arrived on shore, they saw a charcoal fire laid with fish on the grill. He had bread too.

**Jesus** *(to disciples)*: <sup>10</sup>Bring some of the fish you just caught.

<sup>11</sup>Simon Peter went back to the boat to unload the fish from the net. He pulled 153 large fish from the net. Despite the number of the fish, the net held without a tear.

**Jesus:** <sup>12</sup>Come and join Me for breakfast.

*A*fter spending time with Jesus, I realize there are no coincidences. He revealed to me a world where God is intimately involved, the main actor in the drama of history. It was no accident that we caught the fish. It was no accident the nets didn't break. These fish, all 153, were a sign from God representing the community of believers, men and women transformed by faith. Some of us sat down and didn't say a word as we pondered all of this. Others busied themselves in work, their hands moving quickly to stack the catch in baskets and untangle the nets. Each in his own way thought, wondered, and prayed. I have to admit, the prospect of it all still makes me smile.

That's how I always begin and end my stories of Jesus. I remind my little children that through faith He gives us the authority to become the sons of God. Brother Paul said it's all grace. He's right. We are what we are because of His wonderful work in us. The challenge we face every day is to become what we are—His loving, devoted children. To do that, we have to strip away every vestige of our old lives. Like worn out clothes, we find our former lives aren't able to contain the beauty of this new creation. Before we can put on the new life and take up our new calling, we have to set aside every ugly and broken aspect of our lives. Repentance, Jesus told us, is not just about what you put off. It's about what you put on. In the human spirit, there is no vacuum. Something will always occupy you and fill your life. It is either life from above or death from below. If the resurrection of Jesus taught us anything, it's that He is the resurrection and the life. I'm not talking about life after death. What I mean is that through Jesus we can have abundant life, a full and meaningful life, here and now.

Not one of the disciples dared to ask, "Who are You?" They knew it was the Lord. [13] Jesus took the bread and gave it to each of them, and then He did the same with the fish. [14] This was the third time the disciples had seen Jesus since His death and resurrection. [15] They finished eating breakfast.

**Jesus:** Simon, son of John, do you love Me more than these other things?
**Simon Peter:** Yes, Lord. You know that I love You.
**Jesus:** Take care of My lambs.

[16] Jesus asked him a second time . . .

**Jesus:** Simon, son of John, do you love Me?
**Simon Peter:** Yes, Lord. You must surely know that I love You.

**Jesus:** Shepherd My sheep.

**Jesus** (*for the third time!*): [17]Simon, son of John, do you love Me?

Peter was hurt because He asked him the same question a third time, "Do you love Me?"

**Simon Peter:** Lord, You know everything! You know that I love You.

**Jesus:** Look after My sheep. [18]I tell you the truth, when you were younger, you would pick up and go wherever you pleased; but when you grow old, someone else will help you and take you places you do not want to go.

---

*W*hen Jesus took Simon Peter off to the side to speak to him, the rest of us knew what was about to happen. He felt small. He felt he had betrayed Jesus. Up to that point, neither Simon nor Jesus had brought it up. They sat far enough away that the rest of us couldn't hear what was said. We tried to look busy, like we didn't notice. But we did. Simon told us later how it went, what Jesus said. I think that conversation on the beach that day affected him profoundly. From then on, Simon was one of the most humble men I knew.

What got everyone's attention was that Jesus called him "Simon." He hadn't done that in years. From the time that Jesus gave him the nickname "Peter" ("the Rock"), He had always referred to him by that name. But "Peter" hadn't felt like "the Rock" ever since the night Judas betrayed us. For days he felt miserable, like a complete traitor. Jesus knew that, so when it came time to give him "the talk," He called him "Simon."

---

[19]Jesus said all this as an indicator of the nature of Peter's death, which would glorify God. After this conversation, Jesus said,

**Jesus:** Follow Me!

<sup>20</sup>Peter turned around to see the disciple loved by Jesus following the two of them, the one who leaned back on Jesus' side during their supper and asked, "Lord, who is going to betray You?"

*W*hat Jesus did next was nothing short of brilliant. Three times He asked Simon whether he loved Him. Simon was perturbed that Jesus asked him the same question three times. But later he figured it out—with my help, I might add. Three times Simon denied Him. Now Jesus gave him three chances to repent, confess his love, and be restored. Face-to-face with His Lord, he declared his love; and as he did, he felt the burden of his betrayal lift. He began to feel more like the rock he was. Jesus forgave him and then commissioned him to take care of His people. We all took notice. Our Master put Peter, the Rock, in charge.

We all learned a lesson that day. No matter what we have done, no matter the weight of our burden and sin, our Master wants the miracle of forgiveness to restore us to be the people He made us and called us to be. Something happens when we confess our love for Jesus. We are transformed. Our burdens lift. The positive confession of our love for God, hearing His voice, and doing what He asks are as important as confessing our faults.

**Peter:** <sup>21</sup>Lord, and what will happen to this man?
**Jesus:** <sup>22</sup>If I choose for him to remain till I return, what difference will this make to you? You follow Me!

<sup>23</sup>It is from this exchange with Jesus that some thought this disciple would not die. But Jesus never said that. He said, "If I choose for him to remain till I return, what difference will this make to you?" <sup>24</sup>That very same disciple is the one offering this truthful account written just for you. <sup>25</sup>There are so many other things that Jesus said and did; and if these accounts were also written down, the books could not be contained in the entire cosmos.

*I*nitially, all of us stayed in Jerusalem, basking in the glow of the Spirit and the power of His presence. It took a wave of persecution to dislodge us from David's capital and take the message to Judea, Samaria, and the ends of the earth. We really didn't know what to expect. The suffering we faced was a surprise, but we should have anticipated it. Jesus suffered, so why would it be any different for us? What He is showing us is that the fruits of our labor will be so much sweeter when they are rooted in His mission.

He lays out this choice as He did on the beach when He laid fish on the grill: "You can stay here if you want, and drown in grief, spending the rest of your days trying to feed your own hunger. Or you can follow Me, serve My people, and feast on My endless love." What He is saying is that our lives are about more than just feeding ourselves; they're about feeding the world.

I've reached the end of my story. This old man is tired and ready for a rest. It will come soon enough. You'll go on without me, but not without my words. My voice is added to the voices of the prophets and the witnesses. God has become flesh. Somehow this man, Jesus, manifested God's life in our midst. Now that's a pretty big idea for a fisherman. I'll let people smarter than I am figure that one out, but I'll go to my grave bearing witness that it is true.

Now it is your turn to pass along the faith to your children and grandchildren. It's your turn to leave behind your former ways, as we all did, to receive a new life. You have everything you need. You have the Scriptures. You have my account of the good news. You have the church. And you have the Holy Spirit to empower and guide you. You are not alone.

As Jesus prayed for all of us, I pray to God the Father that you will enter into God's kingdom, that faith will grow deep inside you, and that you will experience eternal life. I invite you to join me in this marvelous journey.